Bridge That Gap

How to Get Anything You Want With Conscious Thinking

LEYLA Y MOONE

First published by Ultimate World Publishing 2025
Copyright © 2025 Leyla Moone

ISBN

Paperback: 978-1-923425-35-4
Ebook: 978-1-923425-36-1

Leyla Moone has asserted her rights under the Copyright, Designs and Patents Act 1988 to be identified as the author of this work. The information in this book is based on the author's experiences and opinions. The publisher specifically disclaims responsibility for any adverse consequences which may result from use of the information contained herein. Permission to use information has been sought by the author. Any breaches will be rectified in further editions of the book.

All rights reserved. No part of this publication may be reproduced, stored in or introduced into a retrieval system, or transmitted in any form, or by any means (electronic, mechanical, photocopying, recording or otherwise) without the prior written permission of the author. Any person who does any unauthorised act in relation to this publication may be liable to criminal prosecution and civil claims for damages. Enquiries should be made through the publisher.

Cover design: Ultimate World Publishing
Layout and typesetting: Ultimate World Publishing
Editor: Carmela Julian Valencia

Ultimate World Publishing
Diamond Creek,
Victoria Australia 3089
www.writeabook.com.au

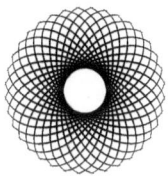

Disclaimer

The following statement serves as a general disclaimer for the book Bridge That Gap by Leyla Moone. This disclaimer is intended for informational purposes and addresses various aspects including personal, medical and financial considerations.

The views, opinions and advice provided in Bridge That Gap, authored by Leyla Moone, are offered as guidance and inspiration based on personal experiences and research. They do not constitute professional advice in any field, including but not limited to personal development, psychology, finance or health. Readers are encouraged to seek advice from qualified professionals regarding their specific situations and needs.

Leyla Moone and associated entities do not assume any responsibility for actions taken by readers based on the information provided in this book. The content is provided 'as is', and while efforts have been made to ensure accuracy and reliability, no guarantees are made regarding the completeness, accuracy, suitability or applicability of the information presented.

Readers are advised to exercise caution and critical thinking when applying concepts or strategies from Bridge That Gap to their lives. Individual results may vary, and Leyla Moone and associated entities disclaim any liability for direct or indirect consequences resulting from the use of this book.

Furthermore, any references to personal, medical or financial matters within the book are provided for illustrative purposes only and should not be interpreted as endorsements, guarantees or promises of specific outcomes.

In cases where readers may be experiencing depression or other mental health issues, it is crucial to seek assistance from qualified healthcare professionals. Bridge That Gap is not a substitute for professional medical or psychological advice, diagnosis or treatment.

This disclaimer is subject to change without notice, and readers are encouraged to review it periodically for any updates or revisions. By accessing and reading Bridge That Gap, readers acknowledge and agree to the terms of this disclaimer.

To my greatest teachers –
my three exceptional children.

Contents

Disclaimer	iii
Foreword	1
Introduction	3
How to Use This Book	7

Part 1: GAP — 11

Chapter 1: Controlled Chaos	13
Chapter 2: Tainted Thinking	33
Chapter 3: Quality Questions	47
Chapter 4: Vivid Vision	65

Part 2: TOOL — 79

Chapter 5: Agile Action	81
Chapter 6: Magnetic Momentum	89
Chapter 7: Make Magic	105
Chapter 8: Present Peace	115

Part 3: THE GIFT — 127

Chapter 9: Constant Change	129
Chapter 10: Final Frontier	137
Chapter 11: Living Legacy	147
Chapter 12: True Transformation	153
Afterword	159
About The Author	161
References	163
3 Offers With Calls To Action	165
Speaker Bio	167

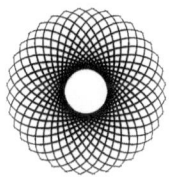

Foreword

Bridge That Gap is a straightforward, instructional guide designed to lead you from where you are now to where you wish to be. And if you don't know where you wish to be, Leyla helps you unravel that mystery as well.

What makes this book truly stand out is Leyla's unwavering dedication to her craft. She has not only poured years of experience, research and personal breakthroughs into these pages, but she has also lived every principle she teaches. Her depth of knowledge, combined with her ability to break down complex ideas into simple, actionable steps, makes Bridge That Gap a practical and powerful resource.

Leyla skilfully interweaves her own life journey in *Bridge That Gap*, demonstrating that she walks the talk. Her resilience, commitment and ability to transform adversity into success are evident throughout the book. This is not just a theory-based guide – it's a tried-and-tested roadmap forged by someone who has put in the hard work and emerged stronger.

As I read through the book, I see my own journey of personal development in its pages. It is a testament to Leyla's ability to connect with the reader, guiding them through their own transformation.

Thank you, Leyla, for inviting me to contribute to this book. I've been a witness to part of your journey, and it is a pleasure to see your development firsthand. Your dedication and passion for helping others shine through in every chapter.

What you will find in Bridge That Gap are ways to do exactly what the title implies. There are exercises explained and demonstrated, which, if the reader puts them into place, will help them create the development they seek in the shortest time possible.

If you are seeking to create powerful change in your life, I suggest that reading this book and practising the wisdom contained within will help you on your own journey, just as it helped Leyla in hers. You are gaining the benefit of the lessons learned by overcoming life's trials and tribulations.

This book should be a must-read for every student of personal development. It's not only a great starting point but also a great refresher for those already on the journey. Leyla's commitment to personal growth and her passion for guiding others make this book an invaluable tool for anyone looking to break through limitations and achieve lasting success.

Here's to your outstanding success!

Wayne Donnelly
Mindset Coach, Hypnotherapist, Speaker

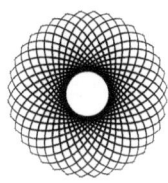

Introduction

This book is your guide to unlocking valuable insights, practical strategies, and actionable steps to transform your life. As we journey through the pages ahead, we'll explore the power of conscious thinking in shaping your present circumstances and expanding the horizons of your aspirations to craft the next few years ahead.

Each moment presents an opportunity to tap into a pool of limitless possibilities. But how do you access this pool and manifest the life you desire? I'll show you how to bridge that gap and achieve anything you wish through conscious thinking. I use the word *thinking* because it is a constant and never-ending activity that all of us engage in every waking moment.

The title of the book invites you to explore the intersection where the art of choice meets heightened awareness. It's about empowering yourself to create a life that brings you happiness and fulfilment.

In a world inundated with information and distractions, it's easy to become a mindless consumer, susceptible to the pressures of **external** influences. But deep down you possess the innate ability to be the creator of your own reality. This is your true nature and purpose. Apologies for the spoiler alert, but the ultimate goal of all that walk this planet is to become the predominant creative force in your life.

My life's work has been dedicated to helping individuals cut through the noise and take on an inward journey of self-discovery. Noise can take many forms – from incessant phone notifications to clutter in our physical spaces to the thoughts that come and go. By cultivating awareness and intentional choices, you can reclaim control over your life and design a future that aligns you with your created vision.

By navigating the landscape of modern life inundated with an abundance of distractions, it's easy to feel overwhelmed and lost. However, amidst the chaos, there lies a profound opportunity for transformation, a chance to reclaim control over our destinies and manifest the lives we truly desire.

Continuing by exploring and clarifying our values, slowly rebuilding trust in our potential selves and shifting our focus towards a life we love every moment, we unravel the tangled web of uncertainty and doubt. Each small step forward, no matter how insignificant it may seem, brings us closer to our aspirations and instils within us a sense of fulfilment and purpose, creating the life we love.

Discipline, determination and decision-making become our allies on this journey of self-discovery. Through the power of conscious thought and intentional action, we unlock the door to endless possibilities and unleash the boundless potential that lies dormant within us.

Let's begin your transformative quest – guided by your inner compass that nurtures your vision daily and fuelled by the promise that anything is possible with conscious thinking. Each moment is an opportunity for growth and every decision shapes the landscape of our reality.

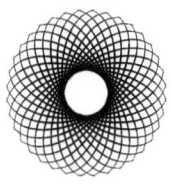

How to Use This Book

At the end of a few select chapters, there are exercises designed to help you gain clarity on your desired result. You will find the exercises grouped under the three parts of the book: Gap, Tool and Gift.

It's best to dive into the exercise as soon as you come across it. After finishing the exercises, you can go back and refine them. If you plan to work your way through this book only once, then do the exercises as thoroughly as possible the first time around. Your life isn't a simple life to be amused by external entertainment. This is what you have already been doing till now. It is, however, a collaborative co-creation to be designed so that you can enjoy the fruits of your labour. As you are already doing this without too much awareness, it's nice to shift perspectives and really be in the driver's seat. Remember, success isn't a far-off destination but a continuous journey where each conscious step forward is a success in and of itself.

A great idea is to keep your initial set of answers from the exercises, allowing you to revisit the process after a period of, say, six months or a year. This way you can assess your progress with each area of your life compared to the previous set of exercises.

BRIDGE THAT GAP

I have found that introducing clients to these exercises helps unleash their potential for a more personally satisfying life. Additionally, repeating the process with a gap in between provides a deeper sense of understanding and insights about you and the concepts you're working through. It also allows you to become your own coach, questioning your purpose and stepping out of your comfort zone on your own terms. This demonstrates that you are gaining confidence, conviction and courage within yourself. And that's what really counts.

Also, by keeping a journal handy, you can note down your thoughts and questions, and if you are a visual person, you can create pictures or other insights that come to you while going through the book to engage the left, rational hemisphere of the brain. Through conscious thinking, what you're really trying to do is reprogram your subconscious mind so that your new way of living in the world becomes habitual, just like brushing your teeth! Every day is different. Life is made up of various emotions, pain and pleasure, dark and light, growth and decay, up down, yin yang – use your own definition of contrast. How you respond to daily life activities will determine your ability to push through while remaining centred and being the **predominant creative force in your life**[1] – in other words, intentionally shaping your own life path.

You are the answer you've been seeking. Embrace the elements around you (earth, water, air and a little clean fire once in a while), feeling the warmth and love emanating from your heart where the real fire resides. That's where the true magic happens. Are you ready to explore your full potential and actively participate in creating a new 2.0 version of yourself?

OK, let's go!

Part 1
GAP

Chapter 1

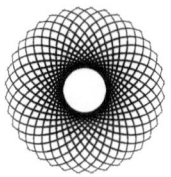

Controlled Chaos

When was the last time you did something for the first time? Seriously, when was the last time you randomly went out and did something that you've never done before? Do you remember the thrill of your first adventure? That sense of wonder, energy and fearlessness?

When we were young there were hundreds, maybe even thousands, of firsts – the first time we walked, first fizzy drink, first sandcastle, first love, first oyster, first job. We saw the world as a place full of wonder, magnificence and a place to conquer. We were all innocent adventurers – full of energy, full of inspiration, and a delight to be around. We were not afraid to try new things even if it was a little daring, like the first time jumping into a pool from a diving board at the local swim centre. We laughed hysterically without any inhibitions, and we were agile, impulsive and sometimes unpredictable. We tried new outrageous dance moves and laughed uncontrollably at one another.

As life unfolded, we moved through the years with ceremonial strides, attending school with a sense of ritual. Day by day, year by year, we found ourselves inexorably shaped by the subtle hand of tradition, unaware of the profound influence it exerted upon us. We became boxed into routines and societal norms, forgetting the joy of spontaneity and exploration.

Without our conscious awareness, we found ourselves immersed in centuries-old frameworks, adhering to the inflexible structures enforced by external systems. These systems were carefully created and upheld to keep us stuck in the surface-level aspects of life, stopping us from exploring the depths of who we really are. That's where our genuine and endless creativity resides, patiently waiting to be seen, acknowledged and let out to play.

Imagine if you were to wholeheartedly embrace life, with curiosity and wonder within you, as if you were a child beginning anew each day. Every day held a new fun activity. Imagine yourself approaching every moment with a thirst for knowledge, living with an open heart, living every experience without fear or inhibition, questioning the workings of the world around you and fearlessly expressing your emotions. Picture letting go of anger effortlessly, releasing any lingering resentments with ease. Picture living with a purity of heart and mind, free from the burdens of negativity. Wouldn't that be truly liberating? It's not about reckless abandon, but about finding the balance between structure and spontaneity.

When you have a vision and are on purpose, then you could live just like that!

It's going to be a little bit tricky at first to become the predominant creative force in your life, since we have gone with the wind and now have all the knowledge at our fingertips.

These days children have heroes that do outrageous things on social media and closely monitor how many likes they have on their chosen application; our psychological well-being is taking on a new shape that is unfamiliar. Adults are also going with the flow, being entertained by the handheld gadget on public transport and shrugging it off as 'catching up', when what it's really doing is taking time away from the things that are more important in life, like being present.

I have found that most people come to a certain age in their adult life and settle for what they're doing in a dull haze of toxic gratitude without pursuing anything further. They are masking a level of gratefulness enveloped in mild fear of change and dismiss their feelings, desires and the persistent signs, settling for less than what they truly wish for.

For instance, if they are continually getting signs that their current job isn't serving them, they would think 'I'm getting paid well', 'Lots of people are out of work, so I should be happy', 'I won't even negotiate for more money' or 'I'm lucky that I get to work from home anyway'. In relationships these thoughts could be 'Nobody's perfect, so I should stay with my partner' or 'It's better than being alone'.

Confronting the Chaos

We encounter challenges that shake us to our core, forcing us to face our realities and make tough decisions. But it's in these moments of chaos that we find clarity and the opportunity for growth.

Several years ago, my life was one big chaotic mess, both in my home environment and in my thinking. I lived in a rundown house where the rent increased yearly, just ended a four-year relationship that was toxic, and I didn't have a great relationship with my children – one child was living with their partner, the other left home at a very young age and at times randomly showed up to stay over, and my third child was not quite sure if he wanted to move wherever I was intending on going. I was doing all that was possible to avoid facing myself and the broken relationship with my family.

I was on the verge of empty nesting and certainly wasn't ready for all this change. I went from being needed, doing things for the family, to not knowing who Leyla was and what she likes and wants to be, do or have. The only stable element in my life was my aptitude for securing employment; I presented well and had a strong resume.

My weekends were taken up with house hunting so that I could get out of my current home of 14 years. I was getting tired of spending my Saturdays from one side of town to the other, not knowing where I wanted to live. I put in an offer for two different apartments at very different localities and then went on a pre-planned holiday to an ashram in India. I continued liaising with the agents via WhatsApp. They asked for significantly more for both the homes I was interested in and asked me to see if the bank would extend the pre-approved loan. Both apartments needed renovations, and if I paid more for the property itself, I wouldn't have had extra funds for improvements. So, I decided to pass on both while settling into the calmness of the ashram for the next three weeks.

Everything back home was a struggle. I was so glad to step away and take a good hard look at the entire situation that I was in, my age, my children's situation, my job, my health, my life and where to from here.

The week I came back from India, still basking in my meditative zen, I thought I'd browse the real estate phone application to see what the property market was doing. An apartment came up that was in an area I avoided and hadn't previously considered. It presented well – neat-as-a-pin unit with three bedrooms, new state-of-the-art kitchen and bathroom, wooden floors throughout, a lock-up garage and a stroll to the shops.

I didn't like the suburb, but I nonchalantly called the agent to see the property that evening just so I could get back to searching for a place to live. The traffic would be heavy after work hours, so I told him I'd be quite late to view the place. The agent arranged with the owner and advised that it was OK for me to view it that evening however late I got to the property, as the agent's office was close by. It took me over an hour to arrive at the unit. As the owners were sitting in the lounge room, I didn't want to intrude, so I walked in, pretty much ran through the place and out very quickly. As I walked out with the agent, he asked me, 'Well what do you think? Do you like the place?'

I immediately fell in love with the home! It was spacious and clean with higher-than-average ceilings. The kitchen was brand new and beautiful. If my children needed a place to stay in the future, I had room for them! This home ticked all the boxes, was 15% cheaper than the other two I looked at before my trip to India, and I could simply move straight in without renovating. I saw myself living here! I made an offer on the contract and handed it to the agent that same night.

The next morning, at 9 am as agreed, he contacted me. After a bit of small talk, he gave me great news that the owner accepted my offer! I was thrilled and relieved that I could stop the search. The entire process unfolded seamlessly right up until the settlement date. I was certain that this place was my next home; it's pleasant in every way and, not to mention, the perfect step along my journey!

Pre-Work – A Life by Design

Reflecting on my journey, I realised how much I had grown since attending my first personal development course. The optimism and knowledge gained from the courses were now being used as I moved through this new period in my life.

When I attended my first two-day weekend personal development course that had come by way of a telemarketing call, I realised how narrow-minded my thinking was. As I listened to others with big dreams who shared their stories, they made drastic changes in their lives that produced great results. I realised their outlook was full of faith. This opened my eyes to this newfound notion of 'creating a life by design'.

I realised the gap between where I was and an elusive, unknown future was massive. There was no future picture that I could even imagine due to the circumstances that I was in at the time. Nevertheless, I attended whatever workshops I could to see what this 'creating a life by design' thing was all about.

The notions that were regularly thrown around in the seminars by many different speakers seemed to be the same things, such as 'Whatever you desire is also seeking you', 'Believe it and you will achieve it', 'Always keep a journal', 'Create a life you love', 'Read your affirmations aloud twice daily', 'Change your money thermostat', 'Look at your vision board every day' and many other common themes. These were ideas reinforced in courses I attended such as T. Harv Eker's and Dr John Demartini's (which I took in November 2013), Bob Proctor's videos and Tony Robbins's UPW event in 2018.

There are numerous methods available to bridge the gap between your current reality and your desired outcome or goal. Personal development teachers offer a plethora of approaches, each tailored to individual preferences. It's essential to articulate your present circumstances in very fine detail, even though it may seem counterintuitive to dwell on them when you're desperately striving to move away from your current situation. This is a crucial step in the process.

Often, when asked about goal-setting practices, many people mention keeping their goals in mind rather than putting them down on paper. However, there's significant power in physically writing down your goals. This act initiates a profound transformation in and of itself, as thoughts transition from the abstract realm of the mind to the tangible realm of paper. Your goals should be clearly articulated on paper or depicted with vivid imagery on a vision board. They should evoke a sense of excitement and energy, motivating you to pursue personal growth and positively impact those around you. I learned this firsthand through PSI 2007 and Life Design Course 2010 with Success and You, which emphasised the importance of setting clear, written goals to unlock personal potential.

Engage emotionally with your goals; this emotional investment creates a powerful vibration. Your energetic frequency influences not only your actions but also what you attract into your life. By aligning your energy with your aspirations, you attract opportunities and circumstances that resonate with your goals, fostering harmony and alignment.

Think → Idea → Result

> **Thinking:** Everything begins with our thinking. Our thinking is the seed from which ideas and actions grow. They are the initial spark of creativity and intention that set the course for our endeavours.
>
> Thinking can be fleeting or persistent, positive or negative, but they all have the potential to influence our perceptions and decisions.
>
> **Idea:** Thinking evolves or coagulates into ideas when they are nurtured and developed. Ideas are the crystallisation of our thinking into more concrete forms. They represent the creative synthesis of mental concepts and may involve brainstorming, problem-solving or conceptualisation.
>
> Ideas provide direction and purpose, guiding us towards specific objectives or solutions. This is the time to write your goals down to solidify them into matter.
>
> **Result:** Ideas, when acted upon, lead to results. Results are the tangible outcomes or manifestations of our

thinking and ideas in the physical world. They can be successes or failures, achievements or setbacks, but they always reflect the culmination of our efforts and intentions. Results provide feedback that informs future thinking and actions, perpetuating the cycle of growth and development.

Thinking is the verb form, indicating the action of using one's mind to consider or reflect on something. *Thoughts* is the noun form, referring to the ideas or mental processes occurring within the mind. So, *thinking* is the action of engaging in cognitive processes, while *thoughts* are the products or results of that mental activity. Personally, I leverage the concept of **thinking** as a potent tool for creation and manifestation.

Current Reality Check

Let's take an honest look at where you are in your life:

1. **Financial Situation:** Take a detailed look at your assets and liabilities. Identify if you're living from your wages week to week compared to your debt. For instance, if you're constantly juggling credit card bills and struggling to cover expenses, then look at your incomings compared to your outgoings.

2. **Emotional Status:** Reflect on your mental state. Assess your mind chatter if you battle anxiety, depression or stress regularly. Consider moments when you feel overwhelmed and on edge. Are you coping with work pressures or personal challenges, or are you at peace within yourself most of the day?

3. **Health Check:** Consider your physical well-being. Acknowledge if you're neglecting physical activity. Notice signs like fatigue, food choices and a balanced lifestyle. Just notice these and write them down as part of your Current Reality Check.

4. **Relationship Desires:** Evaluate the quality of all your connections. Recognise if relationships are fulfilling or leave you feeling isolated. Remember that all connections are relationships and observe how you are presenting yourself with all your communications. Note how your relationship is with yourself. What tone does your mental chatter have? Is it gentle or nasty?

5. **Existential Point of View:** Reflect on your sense of purpose and fulfilment. Notice if you feel stuck in a routine without passion or direction. Acknowledge if you're in a job or situation that doesn't align with your values or if you're experiencing feelings of emptiness despite success.

Brutally examining your current reality and writing it down is crucial for initiating change and regaining control over your life. Use these observations as motivation to start working towards a better future.

Being around people who were transforming their lives was a nice feeling. It filled me with hope and faith for a better tomorrow. On the weekends, I assisted some organisations that welcomed past participants who were familiar with the program to guide newcomers seeking a better way in their lives, which gave me a chance to witness the behind-the-scenes preparation and the extensive planning that went into organising a workshop or a three-day boot camp.

I scheduled a personal appointment with a guest speaker who was a financial advisor. Walking into his boutique office on the North Shore, I felt a bit out of place attending such a meeting. Preparation for the appointment involved presenting my financials and exploring ways to enhance my superannuation fund. With nothing in the fund, he overwhelmed me with details about how a self-managed super fund (SMSF) operates and the exorbitant upfront fee required for his establishment to handle the work. Despite having an accounting background, doing it for myself presented a different challenge. I wasn't familiar with superannuation at all. And how could he justify the fees he was charging? Little did he know the kind of person he was dealing with! Once I set my mind on something, I'm very tenacious, and I have the will to look into it and see it through till the end. I wasn't about to spend money on his services.

Without seeing it at the time, I took a good, hard look at my current reality many times over, realising and reliving repeatedly that my current reality is not where I see myself in five years' time.

I saw superannuation or SMSF as a starting place to change my financial state. I took an evening course on SMSFs for a fraction of the price that was offered by the financial advisor. Other attendees were couples, almost at retiring age, and here I was, in my mid-30s, eager to absorb this information and do this for myself. I set up all the legalities with a small amount in the fund and learned the process.

After taking the evening course I realised the importance of proactive decision-making, and slowly over the next decade I watched the fund flourish. I'm reminded that taking action all those years ago was pivotal in shaping my current financial standing and taught me a valuable lesson about the importance of decisive action.

Holistic Wellness Wheel Exercise – A Snapshot of Your Life in the Present

The Holistic Wellness Wheel is a helpful tool that will guide you forward to adopt a growth mindset. It is a visual representation – or a dashboard, if you will – that shows which areas of life need attention to create harmony and balance and areas you are fully satisfied with and don't need improving.

The goal is to add actionable steps to feel satisfied with each aspect of life. By adding these steps into your week, aiming for a rating of 10 out of 10, you'll improve that part of the wheel. This ensures that your life wheel rolls smoothly when placed on a spoke.

Personal transformation is a dynamic and multifaceted process. It often involves a combination of various tools and practices. Delve into essential tools and practical strategies to bridge that gap that empower us to overcome challenges.

The wellness wheel concept aligns with Tony Robbins's approach to balancing key areas of life for overall well-being.

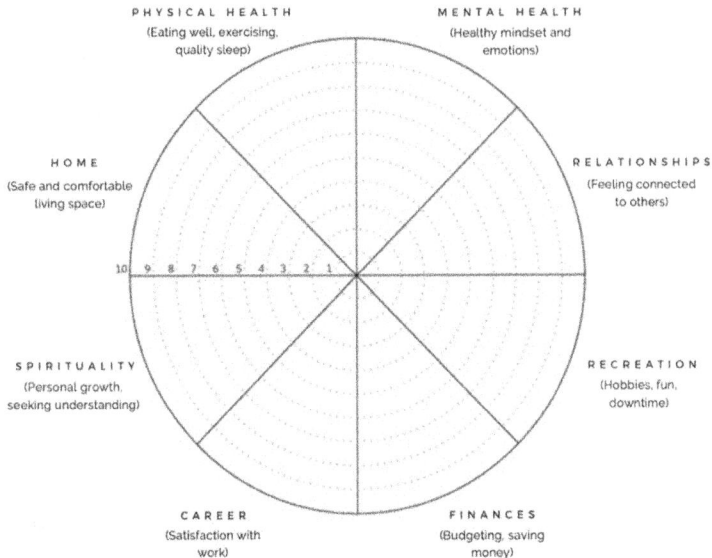

The focus areas are as follows:

1. **Physical Wellness** – Good food. Regular exercise. Quality sleep.
2. **Mental health** – Healthy self-talk. Stable emotions
3. **Relationships** – Level of feeling connected to family friends and colleagues.
4. **Fun/Recreation** – Hobbies. Fun. Social interactions.
5. **Finances** – Budgeting. Saving money. Spending habits.
6. **Career** – Job satisfaction. Location.
7. **Spirituality** – Personal growth. Seeking understanding. Connection.
8. **Home** – Safe. Sacred. Comfortable space

Exercise:

On the wheel diagram, each of the eight sections symbolises a different aspect of your life. Evaluate your satisfaction with each area on a scale of 1 to 10, where 1 indicates struggle and unfulfilment, and 10 signifies satisfaction without much need for improvement. Trust your instincts while assigning these ratings.

Now, shade in the corresponding number of spaces on the wheel, starting from the inside and moving outward based on your rankings. Once completed, you will have a visual representation of your overall life satisfaction across these different dimensions and can ascertain which areas require attention to bring the wheel to or close to a full circle. Like the wheels on a bicycle, you need them to be as full of a circle as possible so that you have a smooth ride!

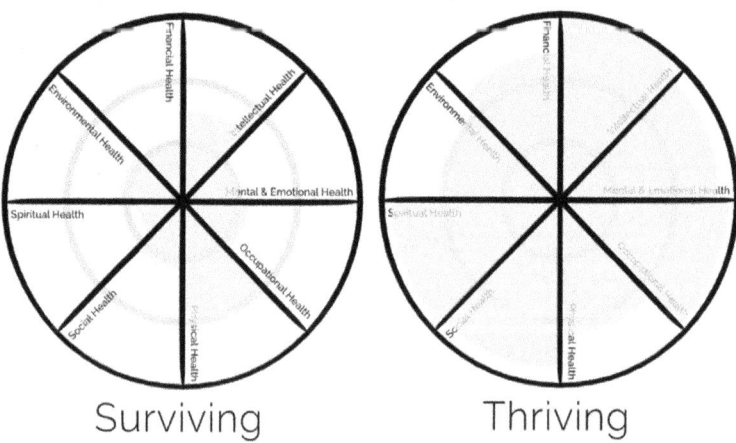

This exercise is good to do once every six months for a check-in with yourself, and you can use it as a dashboard to determine how to improve and score a ten in all categories.

The ways to improve in a certain area can be simple. For instance, if your relationships have a low score, perhaps all you need to do is pick up the phone and make a call to connect with someone. Then, diarise to call or meet up with the person or people to improve the relationships category.

My first health wheel looked like a kite and was very unstable. Although it's not yet a perfect ten for a smooth, rolling wheel, it has certainly improved a lot and now resembles the thriving wheel on the right.

Write down your score for each segment.

Date: ____/____/____
Physical: ____/10 Mental: ____/10. Relationships: ____/10 Recreation: ____/10
Finances: ____/10 Career: ____/10 Spirituality: ____/10 Home: ____/10

Which segments need enhancing to bring it up to a 10? Why?

When you visualise what a 10 looks like within these areas, what images come to mind?

What activities can you see yourself adding to your week to bring this up to a 10?

What action steps can you implement in the next 3–6 months to see a noticeable improvement in these targeted areas?

Whether it's nurturing relationships through regular communication or setting achievable goals for personal growth, the Health Wheel Exercise empowers you to take proactive steps towards a more balanced and fulfilling life. For example, if you have rated the score for your relationships with your parents or siblings at a 4 out of 10, then maybe a phone call locked in your diary every Saturday morning can help strengthen the relationship and bring the score up to a 6 out of 10 within a couple of weeks. It could also involve a half-hour Sunday morning visit to share a cup of coffee with a sibling and make this a regular event to bring the score up a notch. They don't need to know what you're doing; you can keep your personal development goals to better your relationships a secret. They will just feel warmth towards you.

To bridge that gap, assess various areas of your life that you can readily identify and take quick action to thrive not just survive. Dot little actions in your diary for each segment. Through small, actionable steps and increased awareness, you can strategically address each area to bring them up to a ten out of ten.

Harnessing Chaos – A Catalyst for Growth

Chaos can serve as a catalyst for improving your life. By actively participating as a co-creator in shaping the focus areas on the Wellness Wheel, you can explore ways to transmute chaos, fostering creativity, adaptability and agility while cultivating resilience.

The benefits of controlled chaos:

- Keeps your mind sharp.
- Lets you experience less stress.
- Lets you find inspiration anywhere and everywhere.
- Forces you outside your comfort zone.
- Allows you to experience beauty you may have never been able to before, in locations close to home.
- Lets you stay fresh and flexible.
- Makes you adaptable to change.
- Enhances emotional intelligence and intuition.
- Keeps you entertained and makes everyday life fun and enjoyable.
- Gives you the tools to trust your own abilities.
- Increases your belief and trust in yourself.

Unforgettable Lesson in Controlled Chaos – An Insight from My Mathematics Teacher

Amidst the chatter of a typical classroom, an unexpected question from Mrs Bell, my Year 8 math teacher, sparked an unforgettable lesson in controlled chaos.

'What's the quickest way out of the room?' she asked.

BRIDGE THAT GAP

The class engaged in lively discussions, buzzing with a variety of responses for a brief period.

I refrained from any guesses. Instead, I observed the room absorbing the collective insights.

Then in answering her own question, Mrs Bell walked to the farthest corner of the room and, rather rapidly, climbed over the tables and chairs, turning the room into a makeshift obstacle course and made a beeline towards the exit, stumbling and knocking furniture over.

Her unique teaching method, demonstrated through an impromptu obstacle course, taught us a valuable lesson: The fastest route from point A to point B is a straight line, regardless of the challenges that lie on the path to get there.

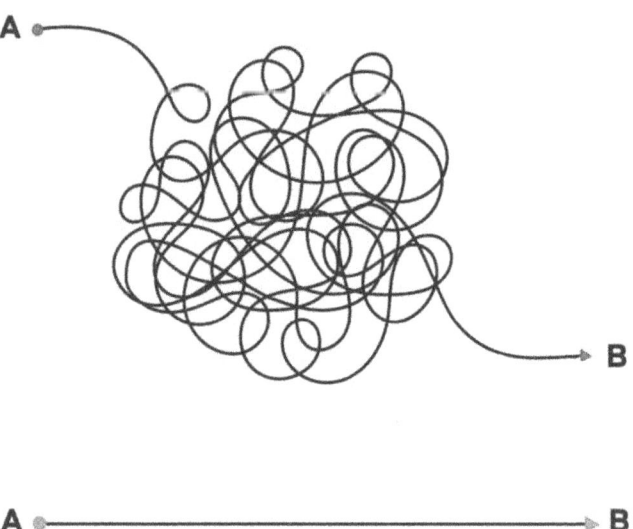

NOTE: In real life situations A to B is never as straight forward as you'd like it to be.

Whenever I catch myself being indecisive about a goal, I channel my inner Mrs Bell! Taking steps to walk a straight line has become my shortcut to clarity, steering away from the emotional roller coaster that looms and swiftly getting back on track. Her unique acrobatic approach might have been entertaining, but the lesson is still used and resonates with me till today.

Chapter 2

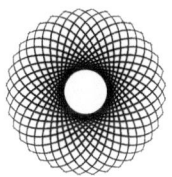

Tainted Thinking

Have you ever thought about thought? What exactly is it and where does it reside? Does it stop when you close your eyes? Have you ever felt that you lack control over the thoughts that are being generated, churned and perpetuated by your mind? Do you notice how different words can alter your emotions? Does your upbringing or past dictate your current thinking process? Does your personality and characteristics influence the thoughts that you think? Does what you allow your eyes to see change your trend of thoughts? To clarify further, when you purposely look at images of the ocean, a flower or a dark figure in a cloak, like a grim reaper, does it alter your thinking process? Is most of your thinking focused on forward planning, worrying about the past or simply being in a present state? Where and when do never-before-thought thoughts come from?

BRIDGE THAT GAP

If you metaphorically take one step back from your thoughts in your mind's eye and become the observer, you can then watch your thoughts as if they are on a movie screen. I know it may sound like a weird concept at first; however, give it a go. Just watch each thought or a group of thoughts rise and subside. They may transition from one idea to another, or you may get triggered by a thought that hooks on to another one and brings up memories, evoking a good or bad feeling.

You may find that by observing your thoughts separately from you, they quieten down a little. It's as if they hush up when they feel like they are being watched – a little like the double slit experiment. I invite you to watch on the internet and fully see what the double slit experiment represents. When particles, like electrons, are shot through two slits onto a screen, they create an interference pattern. But when the experimenter observes which slit each particle goes through, the pattern disappears and the particles act like individual particles instead of waves. In summary, the act of observing changes how particles behave.

Similarly, when we observe our thoughts as separate entities, they tend to quiet down, almost as if they sense being watched. This highlights the powerful impact of observation or meditation on our consciousness and perception.

Our minds wield significant influence. In science, it's recognised that observation, even at the smallest scale such as atoms, can influence and alter behaviour or appearance. This suggests a direct link between our consciousness and the structure of matter. In our daily lives, it stands to reason that it also affects our own behaviour.

Numerous experiments in quantum physics support this concept, establishing it as a fundamental principle. Much research has been done about having a daily meditation practice. It can quiet the mind and relax the body. Additionally, lengthening, drawing out and slowing down your breathing naturally calm the nervous system and help relax the body. This, in turn, quiets an incessantly thinking mind. It also assists in your becoming present.

When we are able to still our thoughts, we come into resonance with the great expanse of a boarder energy. Furthermore, when our mind is quiet and our body is relaxed, we can't be thinking about the future or the past. It's a kind of state of being – we become more aware of our environment and what's happening within our body. Obviously, everyone has a different experience from the one I'm describing, but as a generalisation, our rate of vibration within our body will change.

If we go about our day after adopting a daily meditation practice, whatever we're doing will come not from the mind but from the heart. Poems, artwork, books and any creative endeavours come from this quiet space. It's like tapping into the essence of your inner spirit, achieving a quiet state of mind and embracing the pure presence of your inner being – a vibrational frequency within your body that harmonises with everything else around you. This fine vibrational element also extends beyond your body, transcending physical boundaries to become a conduit for communication between your thoughts and the world around you.

In your awake state, when you decide to meditate, you are consciously deciding to alter your own frequency. How cool is it to know that you can oversee your own state?

BRIDGE THAT GAP

Below is a table of the wave patterns and the corresponding hertz – a unit of frequency measurement. Just notice the tightness of the peaks and troughs in the different waves.

Brainwave Patterns	Frequency	Function	Wave Pattern
Gamma	30 to 100 Hz	Peak performance, flow state, heightened cognitive function	
Beta	12 to 30 Hz	Awake, normal alert consciousness, active thinking	
Alpha	8 to 12 Hz	Relaxed, calm, lucid, not thinking, meditative state	
Theta	4 to 7 Hz	Deep relaxation, meditation, mental imagery, creativity	
Delta	0.1 to 4 Hz	Deep, dreamless sleep, unconscious processes, healing	

Each brainwave frequency plays a critical role in our mental and physical states, influencing everything from alertness to deep restorative sleep. Understanding and optimising these frequencies can enhance cognitive function, relaxation and overall well-being.

It would be exhausting if you were to remain in a gamma frequency throughout the entire day. This prolonged exposure can lead to tightness in the body and a build-up of toxins when not actively purged. It becomes particularly concerning if the only time your mental activity experiences relief is during sleep. This constant high-frequency state without breaks may contribute to physical discomfort and hinder the body's natural detoxification processes.

It's important to incorporate methods, including periods of relaxation, to alter the frequency and achieve calming, lower-frequency mental states daily. How then do we do this? How do we create an imaginary dial so that we are in control of our state?

If you sat in the driver's seat as the captain of your 'body-vessel' and monitored the experiences, you'll notice that various light and sound create different triggers due to their different frequencies. You'll realise that the feeling of love is a long wave, like the delta wave in the diagram, and anger is a short, sharp cycle, like gamma.

The light and sound, along with their intensity all around you, play a role in affecting your thinking and mood. You could say that the thoughts you think are not purely created from you. They are tainted and influenced by your environment via the five senses – sight, smell, sound, taste and touch.

I liken *thinking* to a tube of running water above our heads (or activities in our environment), full of thought forms flowing past in one direction. Your mind has a few fishing lines with hooks on the end of each, flying out above your head and catching random thoughts from the running water.

If you're not aware that your mind is incessantly hooking on to random thoughts, you could be entertained all day long without being productive, just like sitting comatose in front of the television set, watching series after series. Suddenly, five hours have passed and you feel terrible and groggy.

TAINTED THINKING

Once you have a bunch of thoughts being churned by your mind, these thoughts are processed in your body's energetic field in the shape of a torus, also called toroidal field.

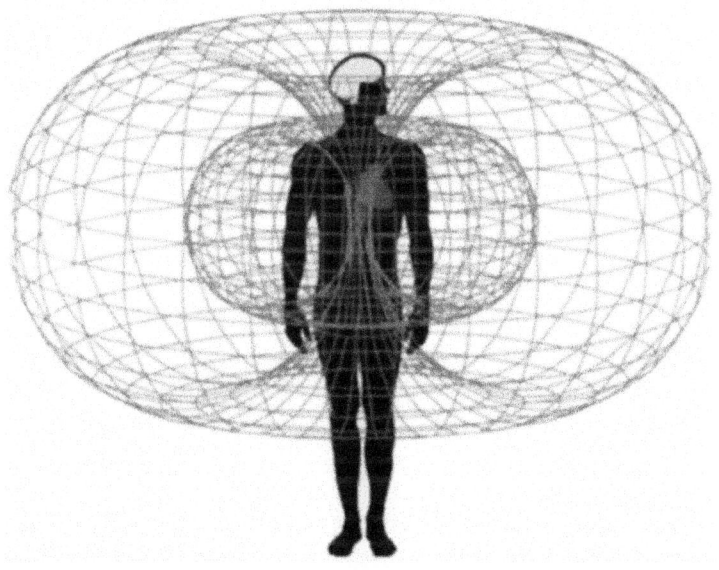

Think of your thought forms as bubbles (high-velocity molecules) being released into the atmosphere. They vibrate and rotate at a divergent range of frequencies within your body's toroidal field and then travel up the centre, to what some have called the Overself – our higher guiding presence, a connection to something greater, a vast universal intelligence like a mainframe of broader consciousness, the collective mind or even the akashic records.

Could it be that our insights and intuition are merely echoes from this greater field of knowing that is beyond the limitations of the individual identity?

This connection – whatever we choose to call it – is our personal link guiding us back to the ultimate God source.

It's as if your physical body is operated by a remote control, with the actual driver being the Overself, which has all the options in its library for you to experience. If you are a conscious thinker, you can pick and choose what you would like to have in your life, steering your life in the direction you choose.[2]

Picture a toy car where the child holds a wired remote control, which controls its movements.

You can liken the Overself to the 'cloud' in computer terminology, where information is stored off your computer. All experiences via the five senses travel upward to be stored in the library of information, just like it's stored in the cloud for a computer.

Inspiration or hunches are messages directly and consciously from the Overself that comes down by way of the Energetic Silver Cord.

Leonardo Da Vinci, renowned for his exceptional artwork, sculptures and sketches, is believed to have been consistently connected with his Overself, infusing his creations with divine inspiration.

The Energetic Silver Cord connects us with our Overself in much the same way as the umbilical cord connects a baby to its mother within the womb. The umbilical cord is a very complex and intricate device, but compared with the Energetic Silver Cord, it is like a cotton thread.[2]

TAINTED THINKING

The Energetic Silver Cord is a mass of vibration rotating over an extremely wide range of frequencies. It is intangible like a tornado in the sea; widely dispersed and unable to be seen by the average sight. It's akin to a tight beam of radio waves. This is the method by which the Overself communicates with the body on earth.

As a very general description, when you do a good deed, you and those around you vibrate at a higher level; that is, you increase your rate of vibration here on earth and it sends good vibes to your astral Overself, increasing the rate of vibrations to give you more of the same good stuff. Whereas, doing an ill deed to someone decreases or subtracts from your rate of spiritual vibration. You lower your vibration and attract more of that lower energy in your days and weeks, experiencing a succession of bad or grey days, perpetuating more of the same.

So, if we return good vibrations in place of a bad deed done to us, as a rule, we will always progress upwards and never downwards and have good life experiences. It's all a matter of vibration, all a matter of what the body transmits by way of the Energetic Silver Cord to the Overself and what the Overself sends back again by way of the Energetic Silver Cord to the body.

> Overall, thinking can be tainted by external influences, unconscious patterns and spiritual energies, so it's important to have a purging process to shake thoughts out of your energetic toroidal field on a daily basis. Go for a brisk walk. Do dynamic breathwork. Swim in the ocean. Swimming in the ocean is actually one of the best and fastest ways to reset the body's energetic field due to the cleansing properties and high vibration of sand and salt in the sea.

Be the Gatekeeper of Your Mind

Be the gatekeeper of your mind in what you allow your senses to experience and adopt a level of conscious awareness in the way your brain processes information. It's fascinating to slow down and be the observer.

I have given you my own interpretation and understanding of our connection to the higher self. Here it is in summary:

1. **Thought Formation:** Thoughts are processed within the body's energetic toroidal field, attached like bubbles around the body before traveling to the Overself (cloud).

2. **Observation and Calmness:** Observing thoughts from a detached perspective can quiet the mind, similar to the effects of meditation and relaxation techniques.

3. **Meditation and Present Awareness:** Engaging in daily meditation enhances present-moment awareness, promoting a quieter mind and deeper connection to surroundings.

4. **Frequency Impact:** Different frequencies influence mental states and emotions, shaping the quality of thoughts and perceptions.

5. **External Influences:** Thoughts are influenced by external factors such as past experiences, sensory inputs and environmental stimuli.

6. **Role of the Overself:** Often described as one's true self or divine essence, the Overself connects to a broader consciousness beyond individual identity. It serves as a conduit for divine inspiration and intuition, guiding experiences and creative expressions.

7. **Energetic Silver Cord Connection:** Symbolising the link between the physical body and the Overself, the Energetic Silver Cord – like an umbilical cord – serves as a conduit for communication and energy exchange.

8. **Growth:** A clean toroidal field, influenced by actions, determines the quality-of-life experiences, with positive vibrations leading to progression upwards fostering well-being and positive life experiences.

True Story

When I was around 12, I had an uncanny ability to guess what song was playing on my parents' clock radio before my sister and I even walked through the front door from school. It became a fun ritual between us – she'd say, 'Guess what's on?' and I'd call it out, almost always getting it right.

I'm not sure what frequencies I was tuning into back then, but to this day I have a continuous ringing in my ear that I can tune in and out of, almost like a built-in signal, helping me sense whether things around me are OK or not.

Discussion Question:

Is there an intriguing ability you had when you were younger that you've lost touch with – or perhaps rediscovered in a new way?

You Are
Born of wisdom, light and sound
Guided held, forever found
No start, no end, just waves that flow-
Feel it now, you simply know

~

Chapter 3

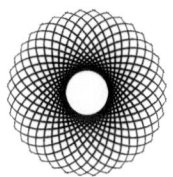

Quality Questions

Our minds are finely tuned problem-solving engines. Present it with a challenge, pose a question, and watch as its innate curiosity sets off a captivating process. With a question, it won't be catching random thoughts and entertaining you all day. It will be conditioned by the questions asked and work hard for you to find answers you seek to resolve.[3]

Think of it as an open energy vortex hovering above your head, reaching out into the ether, past the rushing river of random thoughts. With complex problems, we find ourselves wondering about them for days, immersed in the quest for a solution, unlocking the mysteries that captivate our intellectual journey. This is your mind on a mission.

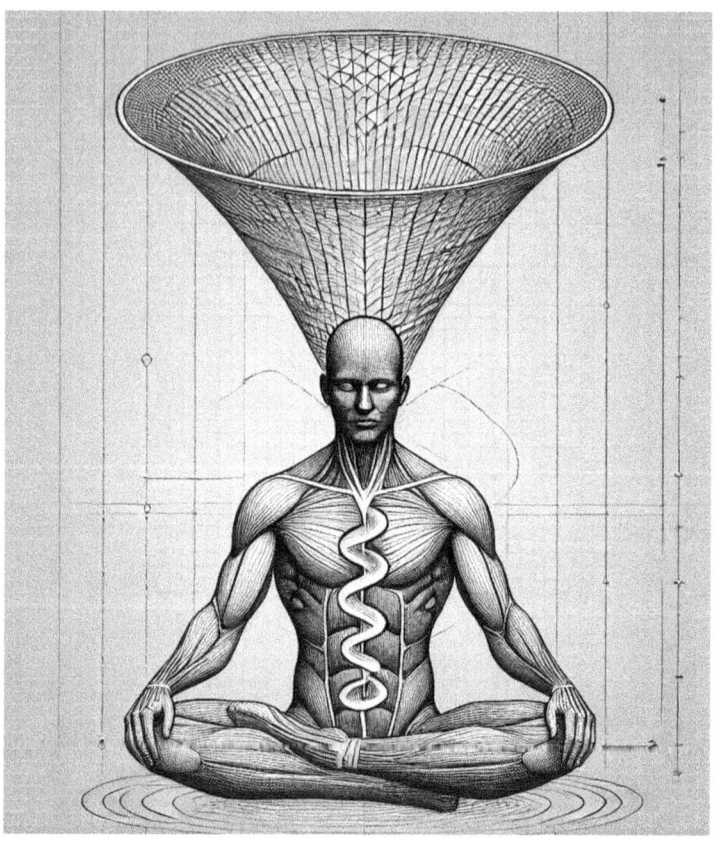

Mechanics of Asking Good Quality Questions

The **Reticular Activating System** (RAS) is a part of the brain that acts as a filter for incoming information, like a gatekeeper in the brain, helping us to stay alert and prioritising what it deems important.

Imagine the RAS as a bouncer at a club with strict entry rules. Only people who have registered and have a QR code can enter the party (your conscious awareness). The bouncer (RAS) scans each QR code, filtering out the uninvited guests (irrelevant stimuli) and allowing the VIPs (important information) with valid QR codes to enter. This helps you stay focused and alert, ensuring that your brain pays attention to what truly matters.

This phenomenon is often referred to as the **frequency illusion**, where something you've just learned or focused on suddenly seems to appear everywhere in your environment.

Now, what are the mechanics of a question that will assist our RAS in bringing a tangible result into our lives? Good quality questions direct our minds to focus on a resolution. Two fundamental words that will keep our thinking in a state of child-like wonder are questions that begin with *Why* and *How*. It will metaphorically keep the energy vortex above our heads open.

Let's visit the concept of activating our thinking:

1. Starting questions with *Why* can lead to confusion. When we ask 'Why?', we may find ourselves in a maze of uncertainties without a clear path forward. This can leave us feeling bewildered by the complexities we encounter along the way. Keep this in mind as we further explore later in this chapter.

2. Beginning questions with *How* brings a sense of method and order to our inquiry. Asking 'How?' prompts a structured and systematic approach to unravelling life's mysteries. It encourages us to delve into processes and engage in disciplined exploration, leading us to practical and tangible understanding.[4]

If you're trying to encourage your mind to resolve a question, it's best to ask lofty questions beginning with the word *Why*.

By posing a question beginning with *How*, it activates your mind to resolve it from the time you ask the question.

> **IMPORTANT:** We need to stay in the space of wonder for a while to encourage the mind to be frazzled and hazy to bring about its genius! Simply put, when you're confused, you're grappling to resolve and learn from the question posed!

If you look at Neurolinguistic Programming (NLP)[5], a psychological approach that involves analysing strategies used by practitioners and applying them to reach personal goals, you'll find that NLP brings about relatively fast changes in thought patterns and behaviour. Practitioners often use rhetorical questions as a tool to challenge and stimulate the mind, prompting individuals to discover their own answers and insights. There are many key principles for its effectiveness, including pattern recognition, anchoring and language, and communication patterns, just to name a few.

Have you ever observed what conversations go on in your head or what pops up in your mind when you've got a minute of quiet time? All sorts of topics come and go, and you hook your attention to a particular thought. For instance, if you had a conversation with someone that day, then your thinking takes on a different trajectory and this mind chatter goes on and on and on!

QUALITY QUESTIONS

Why so? What is your mind doing with all this information or data rolling past? Where is it cataloguing and storing all this churning? Sometimes it's a menace unto itself. According to brain researchers, we think 60,000 thoughts a day (some studies quote more). However, this translates to 11 million bits of information per second by our five senses. Not going into too much detail, but as per the NLP Communication Model, we distort, delete and generalise this data. Otherwise, if we don't delete non-vital information, we'd literally go insane! Our conscious mind can only deal with 100 bits per second.

A *bit* is the basic unit of information, the smallest unit of data in computing and digital communications. It is a binary digit, meaning it can represent one of two values: typically, zero or one.

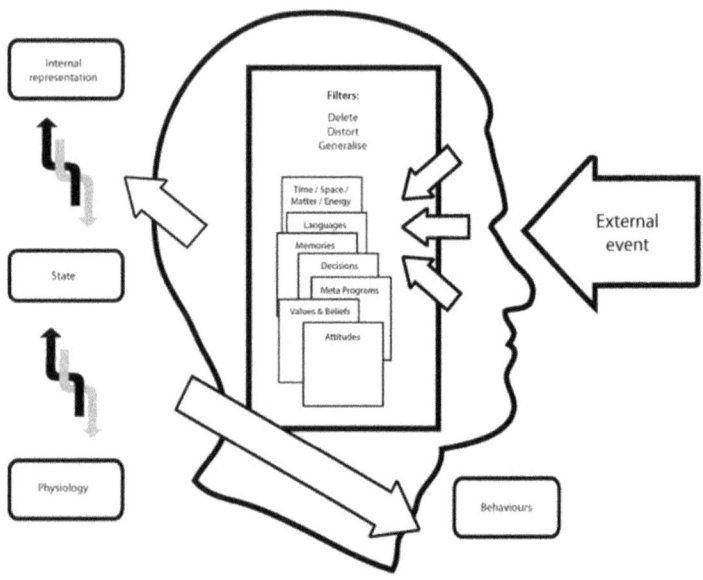

When we step back and take a broader view of how we are playing out in the world, we can take ownership and become the predominant creative force in our lives. Taking back this power and **creating with purpose** is within all of us. Now it's just sitting dormant, waiting for a little bit of attention with our heightened awareness.

Continuing with the mechanics of asking quality questions, positively phrased questions serve to light the way for our minds to organically come up with the resolution. These questions are designed not to confuse but to empower our inquisitiveness, not to mystify but to offer clarity. We'll continue to explore the art of posing questions that encourage helpful answers and also unveil insights by our inquisitive minds.

Note: It's important to mention that the questions do not need answering! They only need to entice curiosity, growth and the transformative power of seeking understanding. Our mind will open a portal, and it's our job to remain in a state of wonder for a while!

Benefits of Lofty Questions and How They Work

Good-quality questions evoke positive feelings. Conversely, if our minds encounter poor-quality questions, the responses will be equally powerful. Be careful what you wish for! Lofty questions go beyond mere inquiry; they actively promote positive identity changes within our subconscious minds. This transformative process aids in overcoming stuck emotional states and effectively brings a desired state into being.[4]

Specifically designed to unlock creative answers within our subconscious, lofty questions foster intuition, insight and a shift in focus. These transformative elements contribute to a different life experience, empowering us to act, solve problems and operate at a higher vibrational frequency.

By encouraging us to explore exciting possibilities, lofty questions facilitate a shift in our perspective and meaning concerning various life situations. They serve as a powerful tool to replace unhelpful negative thoughts with constructive alternatives. Just remember to stay in a state of wonder; it's a safe place for your mind to be!

5 Keys to Creating and Using Lofty Questions.

1. Always phrase the question in the positive.

2. Start with the word *why*.

3. Use the words *always* or *at all times*.

4. Ensure you are asking these questions in a relaxed and meditative state.

5. Repeat as many times as you can to evoke a fountain of gratitude and a feeling of strength and 'unstoppableness' – yes, I made that word up!

An example of a lofty question is 'Why am I always so happy and positive all of the time?'. Another way to pose the question is in the third person, such as 'Why is Leyla always so happy and positive all the time?'. Posing questions in the third person can be powerful for many reasons; one being directive, especially considering the new notion that we live in a hall of mirrors or a holographic world. Stating in the third person provides the following:

1. **Objective viewpoint:** Third-person questions offer an objective and detached perspective, reducing emotional bias.

2. **Neutral observation:** Distance from the question promotes impartial analysis, leading to more rational insights.

3. **Enhanced self-reflection:** Evaluating behaviour as an outsider prompts deeper self-reflection. We are

naturally drawn to helping someone from outside our circle.

4. **Deeper understanding:** A third-person stance reveals hidden patterns or tendencies in one's actions or emotions.

5. **Empowerment:** Analysing oneself externally empowers proactive personal growth and positive change.

6. **Shift in perception:** Third-person questioning aligns with the interconnected nature of experiences.

If your mind keeps asking questions such as:

1. Why am I so broke?

2. Why am I so unlucky?

3. Why is life so hard?

4. Why does this always happen to me?

5. Why do I seem to be unable to live the life of my dreams?

With these thoughts to be resolved by your mind, you'll likely experience financial difficulties, misfortune and hardship because that is what is radiating from your thoughts! Like attracts like.

Good-quality lofty questions frazzle the subconscious mind and reduce cognitive dissonance; they quieten the voice in your head and open threads of attractor patterns or creative genius to come into your life. When you're confused, your mind is seeking a tension resolution, and that's when you truly begin to learn. We will do this in a controlled way for a certain outcome.

Good-quality lofty questions offer a roadmap, guiding you towards living the life you wish to step into.

Exercise:

To help you understand how the subconscious mind works and why lofty questions are so effective, I encourage you to recall a time when you really wished for a particular item, whether it be a push-bike, a dress, a car or a holiday to a certain destination, *fill in the blank*. You allocated a significant portion of your mental space to it, and it consumed your days. You envisioned riding it, wearing it, sitting in the driver's seat or feeling the ocean breeze on your face. You cultivated **faith** and **affirmed** that you **will** have this thing.

You then see that your classmate owns the exact same bike. You notice the dress you like in the shop window, the car you desire is owned by many people on the road and the travel agent has a special on your holiday destination.

Why and how does this work? This kicks in the RAS. With reference to lofty questions, your mind begins seeing reasons and events that match with the question you've posed and attract them into your periphery.

Power Questions

Below are some great lofty questions that you can use in different areas of your life.

Personal:

Why am I always surrounded by happiness and joy all the time?

Why am I always able to learn positively from any experience all the time?

Why is my life always so amazing that it exceeds all my expectations all the time?

Why do I always use what is happening in my life to become a better person all the time?

Why do I always do the right thing for my mind and body all the time?

Relationships:

Why am I always surrounded by incredible, authentic and loving people whom I feel a deep bond with wherever I go all the time?

Why am I always surrounded by people who love, support and respect me all the time?

Why am I always so good at attracting the perfect friends for me all the time?

Money and abundance:

Why do I always have more than enough money to pay the bills, save for my future goals and have lots of leftover money for fun activities all the time?

Why am I always so good at making, keeping and multiplying money, currency and wealth all the time?

Why do I always find new and exciting ways to increase my income all the time?

Why do I always make choices that lead to increased wealth and prosperity all the time?

Why do I always attract financial blessings from unexpected sources all the time?

Productivity:

Why am I always able to do so much in so little time?

Why am I always so great at managing my time so efficiently?

Why am I always focused and in flow while working all the time?

Why do I always actively and easily seek help and collaboration?

Why do I always embrace change for continuous Improvement all the time?

Health:

Why am I always so good at looking after my health and knowing exactly what my body needs from me all the time?

Why do I always make time for daily exercise?

Why do I always maintain a calm and focused mindset all the time?

Why am I always craving healthy whole foods all the time?

Goal achievement:

Why do my goals always come to me so quickly, easily and effortlessly all the time?

Why do I always take effective action towards achieving the life of my dreams?

Why am I always achieving top results within regular work hours all the time?

Why do I bring together the deposit for my investment property so easily and effortlessly?

Why do I always adapt and evolve my goals as needed all the time?

Guidance:

Why am I always so brilliant and so able to develop creative ideas through my intuition all the time?

Why am I always connected to a source of inspiration greater than myself all the time?

Why do I always attract supportive and like-minded individuals into my life all the time?

Why does the universe always give me more than enough health, vitality and energy to reach my goals?

Why do I always recognise and follow the path that leads to my fulfilment all the time?

Imagine now saying something like, 'I'm not anxious.' Your conscious mind will contemplate anxiety, pondering what it feels like to be anxious. You might visualise it in your mind, enabling you to process and subsequently shift your focus towards thoughts of not being anxious. This process can be quite laborious.

Instead, if you use the question 'Why am I always so relaxed?', your brain now thinks about the word *relaxed*. Or when you ask 'Why do I always have courage?', your thinking focuses on courage and ways that you are courageous. Other examples include 'Why am I always so peaceful?' and 'Why am I always so confident?'.

Shift in perspective: When you have positive phrases and positive lofty questions, the unconscious mind will then elevate in wonder and stay open to alternatives.

Daily Affirmation of Quality Questions

Step 1: Craft your quality questions from each of the above categories so that they resonate with what you'd like to see in your surroundings, then write them clearly on a paper so that you can easily read them.

Step 2: Set aside a few minutes each day for this exercise, preferably in the morning or right before bed when you're winding down and your mind is impressionable so that you can focus without distractions.

Step 3: Make sure your space is quiet and comfortable where you can relax and concentrate. Take a few deep breaths to centre yourself and clear your mind.

Step 4: Repeat each of your chosen quality questions out loud, one at a time, slowly and deliberately. Feel the words as you say them and visualise the desired outcome or feeling associated with each question.

Step 5: After reciting each question, take a moment to reflect on it and internalise its meaning. Imagine yourself experiencing the outcome described in the question.

Step 6: Affirm with faith. Repeat your list of quality questions twice daily for maximum effectiveness. Consistency is key to reprogramming your subconscious mind and activating your RAS.

Step 7: If your circumstances change, then tweak the list of questions to suit the changes in your life as needed. Make them upbeat and ensure they make you feel amazing and energised to start and end your day.

Step 8: Conclude the exercise by expressing gratitude for the positive outcomes you've affirmed through the quality questions. Believe in the power of your mind to attract these experiences into your life.

Repetition: 30-Day Challenge

Affirm your list of good-quality questions aloud twice daily, infusing the image in your mind with faith to activate this new trend of thinking and gain a fresh perspective filled with wonder. This aligns your thoughts with your goals and collapses time in your mind's eye, flooding you with the feeling that you already possess those things. It fosters clarity, purpose and positivity.

By making this a morning and nightly habit or ritual, you reinforce these affirmations, embedding them into your subconscious mind and priming yourself with determination. This practice also cultivates a powerful and unshakable inner dialogue that steers your daily actions towards your new standards. To stay on track, use a calendar to cross off 30 days for this challenge, visually marking your progress and boosting your inner strength.

Chapter 4

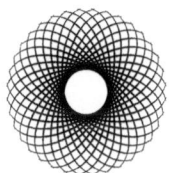

Vivid Vision

Have you ever felt like you're drifting through life without a clear sense of direction? Like you're stuck in a rut, unsure of where you're headed or what you truly wish to achieve? Perhaps you've experienced moments of doubt, wondering if your dreams are nothing more than a distant desire or fantasy. If so, you're not alone with this.

In today's fast-paced world, it's easy to get caught up in the rat race of daily life, losing sight of our deepest wishes and aspirations. We find ourselves going through the motions, living from one day to the next without a clear purpose for the future. And as time goes by, the gap between where we are and where we wish to be seems to grow wider and wider, leaving us feeling frustrated and unfulfilled.

BRIDGE THAT GAP

What if I told you that there's a way to bridge the gap from where you are to where you desire to be? What if I told you that you have the power to turn your dreams into reality? That's where the power of creating a vivid vision in your thinking comes in.

I have found that creating a vision for your future can be the key to unlocking your full potential and turning your dreams into reality. You can create a roadmap for success and inspire yourself to take action towards what you wish to see in your life. You can do this by:

1. clearly defining your goals

2. creating a vision board, a visual representation

3. looking at your vision board a few minutes a day

4. adding feel-good 'e-motion' – energy in motion – while looking at images

5. seeing your ideal result in your mind's eye

6. saying your goals out loud.

Think of your vivid vision as a blueprint for your life, a detailed plan that outlines exactly what you desire to achieve and how you plan to get there. When you have a clear vision of your goals and aspirations, you become more focused, motivated and driven. You start to see opportunities where others see obstacles, and you become more resilient in the face of challenges. Just by having this little secret tool, you feel more confident, have more conviction in yourself and cultivate courage.

But creating a vision for your life isn't just about wishful thinking or positive affirmations; it's about tapping into the power of your subconscious mind to align your thoughts, beliefs and actions with your deepest desires. When you consistently visualise your goals with clarity and intensity, you send a powerful message to your subconscious that these outcomes are not only possible but inevitable.[6]

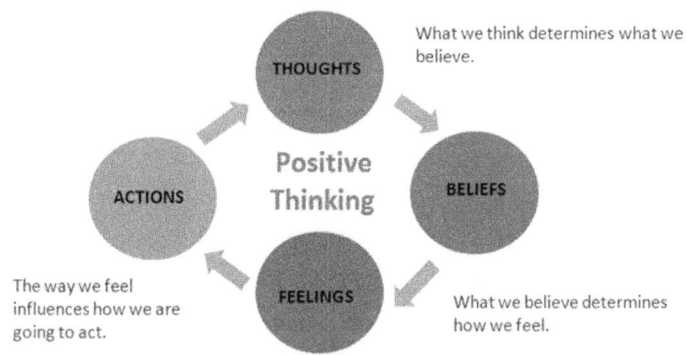

Research tells us that when we practice a new habit repeatedly, our neural pathways and nerve cells can create a habit that becomes natural, just like brushing your teeth. Wouldn't you like to go for a walk every day without the resistance creeping in?

Mental activity strengthens neural pathways; if you're stressed in your thoughts and feelings and don't have mechanisms to snap out of it or change your state, then you strengthen the stress pathways in your brain.

When I was in Boston, I noticed that the streets didn't seem well planned. Later, I learned from the travel guide that they decided to make the main roads of the city on the actual well-trodden cow tracks – it was firm and predictable! It took decades, maybe even centuries, for the cows to create these smooth paths, so the city planners used the path of least resistance to establish the road network!

Just like all new skills that we set out to learn, the habits that we want to see in our lives need a little extra attention at the beginning. The habit of getting dressed at the age of 50 years old is a well-worn pathway that starts at the age of 5. So, the little extra attention at the beginning of a newly decided habit will set it in motion and ensure that it runs on autopilot daily without encountering much resistance.

Numerous studies have shown that seeing your goals on the movie screen of your mind's eye for a continuous 17 seconds activates the same neural pathways in your brain as if you performed the actions required to achieve those goals.[8] This means that your brain does not know the difference between imagined and real action. So, by consistently visualising your desired outcomes, you can prime your brain for success. This deliberate act of visualisation can be used as the perfect tool for lasting impact and permanent change.[7]

One study conducted by Dr Alan Richardson, a renowned sports psychologist, found that athletes who visualised themselves performing their sport in vivid detail were able to improve their performance significantly compared to those who did not do the exercise. Similarly, a study published in the Journal of Experimental Social Psychology found that students who visualised themselves achieving their academic goals were more likely to succeed academically than those who did not visualise.

As my youngest son was in his last year of high school, he saw school as a waste of time and wasn't engaged in studies at all. He just wanted to finish the last few months and go to a technical college. While I dropped him off to school every day, I decided to see if he was open to test something out as an experiment. Since mathematics was his favourite subject, only because he liked the teacher, I asked him what result he thought he might get. His answer was 30 out of 100. I asked what he would like to get. It was tough to get an answer out of him, but he said he'd like to at least pass. After a lot of back and forth, he said that it would be great if he got 70%. OK, we were making progress; 70 is better than a pass! So, without doing any more homework or changing any of his routines, I asked him to repeat the following phrase with excitement twice every day, once in the morning and once before bed: 'I got 70 for my final maths exam'.

As the school year was coming to a close, I'd check in every so often with him to see if he was doing his little experiment, which he was.

I was anticipating how the experiment affected his maths results. When the letter finally arrived, I was so happy and excited to see his final mathematics score! He got 69%! I couldn't help but feel a sense of satisfaction. Though the score was just shy of his target, the improvement from his initial expectations was directly due to the power of creating a positive vision and self-belief. In hindsight, I wish I had done this exercise with all three of my children from the start of school.

By harnessing the power of your imagination, you can overcome self-doubt, boost your confidence and unleash your full potential.

Some people just seem to have that special **Midas touch** – whatever they attempt seems to magically and simply work out to be a great success. I believe that these individuals are masters at intentionally or unknowingly holding a vision of the thing they wish to bring about in their minds so steadfastly, that eventually they become masters at co-creation and what they think about materialises easily and effortlessly.

Donald Hebb's breakthrough discovery in 1949 that 'neurons that fire together wire together' can be used to our advantage to form, strengthen and solidify our neural pathways to fire more of the same synapses. By doing a positive action repeatedly, it becomes familiar to your physiology to repeat it without hassle.

Exercise:

Creating a mental movie screen projected from the middle of your forehead or from the third eye requires some practice to clearly visualise images. Start by closing your eyes and focus on the centre of your forehead, allowing them to naturally close and become slightly crossed. Envision the desired outcome right in front of your forehead, like a small cloud containing a mental picture of your wish. With continued practice, you'll improve your ability to visualise. It's like exercising a muscle within your body – the more you practice, the stronger and more effortless it becomes to manifest your thoughts into things.

After creating a clear mental picture, add some happy emotion; for instance, a smile or a firm 'Yes!' or jumping up and down with joy. This is super important, as this is the gateway to turn your thoughts into real-life things. All great teachers relay this information about turning thoughts in your mind's eye into things by infusing emotion into the exercise. It's like giving it an electrical charge by consciously popping it into your thinking several times a day. Through discipline, you will start to alter the canvas a little to change the trajectory of your future.

Note: I'd like to point out that the third eye is not a physical eye but a focus point and more of a symbol for intuition, deep understanding and connecting to something bigger than ourselves. When you activate this third eye, it's like opening a door to see things more clearly and tap into your creative abilities.

As we age, the distance between where we are and what we aimed for in our youth seems to grow wider, and it becomes harder to bridge that gap, leaving us feeling frustrated and unfulfilled. While it certainly isn't impossible, you'll have to be extra present in strengthening your vision as you go about your day – whether when you're commuting to work, for example, or driving in the car. This repetitive strengthening exercise will show you that the source of the predominant creative force in your life is within you! Leave the noisy and captivating external influences and focus on your inner self, because it's much more fun and rewarding to be creating your life.

I found myself practising vivid vision unknowingly when I decided I'd like to take a course by my favourite author at the time, Robert Fritz, after reading his book Creating and the Path of Least Resistance. I reached out to his office in America to see if they offer courses in Australia so that I can participate in two immersive courses. Sadly, they replied that it wasn't on their agenda anytime soon. I desired it so badly that I added fuel to my vision daily, ultimately resulting in taking his courses in America for two years in a row.

While my first trip was scary and quite stressful, on the second trip I took an Amtrak train from Los Angeles to New York. Then, I decided to hire a car and drove from Hartford to New York, then to Boston, and finally to Vermont – never having driven on the opposite side of the road as we do in Australia. Confusion hit me every time I came to a roundabout or on long stretches of the road. I'd slightly swerve on the side of the road that I was used to! Luckily the Americans are friendly people. They would honk the horn to assist me on my trip. What more could I ask for! Looking back, I don't know where I found the courage! I give myself credit for just going and staying laser-focused on something I desired to do!

The phenomenon of looking at a vision board daily and writing down what you desire in intricate detail repeatedly and with focused intent sets a powerful process in motion. Things unfold as the same threads of consciousness filter down from our thinking and weave through our thoughts and through our body that then materialise into the fabric of our existence.

A friend of mine, who had a crystal-clear vision and unshakeable belief, created a vision board with a few keywords and some simple sketches and wrote about her dream sales job in another state. Despite being in accounting, her unwavering conviction that her new sales role had already materialised in her life became the driving force. She applied for many jobs. Her new sales career unfolded unexpectedly through an old colleague she hadn't seen for several years. A casual phone call seamlessly made the connection between vision, belief and the tangible manifestation of her dream and real life. She went on to buy a unit and happily moved to create a new life for herself.

My first vision board during that first two-day personal development weekend was a spiral of images ranging from landscapes to products to portraiture. I loved photography and aspired to do it all! As there was no focus on one area, my photography business was just that – a mish-mash of photography work that made no money and ended up in chaos and financial mess, just like the picture spiral collage that the vision board represented. Be careful what you wish for!

Clarity in expressing our desires is very important, as the universe tends to respond to the precision with which we express our wishes. 'Be careful what you wish for' serves as a cautionary reminder, highlighting the significance of understanding the consequences that accompany our desires.

Our thoughts and intentions carry a strong distinct energy, capable of shaping our reality once expressed. Hence, it becomes crucial to articulate with care, ensuring that our wishes align authentically with our truest intentions and contribute positively to both our lives and the lives of those around us.

Today my vision boards are clear and clean, with only a few images. Once I achieve what I initially aimed for, I then create a new vision board to focus on. I will keep creating them, as they strengthen my belief that we create our lives.

Vision Board Exercise

Here's a detailed, step-by-step vision board exercise for both digital and physical vision boards:

Step 1: Set the scene

Begin by finding a quiet and comfortable space where you can focus without distractions. It could be on the floor or a study desk. Prepare all your materials in advance, whether you're making a digital vision board or using magazine cutouts for a physical board.

Step 2: Reflect and visualise

Take a few moments to reflect on what you wish to pursue to see in your life in 12 months, 3 years and 5 years' time. What are your dreams and aspirations? Close your eyes and visualise your ideal future. What does success look like to you? What are your biggest dreams and desires? Allow yourself to dream big and imagine the life you truly wish to live.

Step 3: Choose your focus

Decide on a specific theme or focus for your vision board. It could be career goals, health and wellness, relationships, travel or personal development. Select images and words that align with your chosen theme and inspire you to take action towards your goals.

Step 4: Gather inspiration

For digital vision boards, browse through websites like Pinterest or Google Images to find pictures and quotes that resonate with you. Save these images to your computer or device. For physical vision boards, grab a stack of magazines and start flipping through them to find images and words that capture your vision.

Step 5: Get creative

Now it's time to get creative! If you're making an online digital vision board, open a blank canvas on a platform like Canva or even PowerPoint and start arranging your images and quotes. Experiment with different layouts and colours until you find a design that speaks to you. If you're using a physical board, grab a piece of cardboard or poster board and start arranging your magazine cut-outs using glue or tape.

Step 6: Add personal touches

Inject your personality into your vision board by adding personal photos, handwritten quotes or other meaningful items. Make it uniquely yours, and make it something that will inspire you every time you look at it.

Step 7: Display and take action

Once your vision board is complete, find a prominent place to display it where you'll see it every day. Whether it's hanging on your wall, saved as your desktop background or pinned to your fridge, make sure it's somewhere you can easily access. Finally, commit to taking action towards your goals every day. Use your vision board as a daily reminder of what you're working towards, and let it inspire you to take steps towards making your dreams a reality.

Remember, the most important part of creating a vision board is taking action. Let your vision board be a catalyst for positive change in your life.

Part 2

TOOL

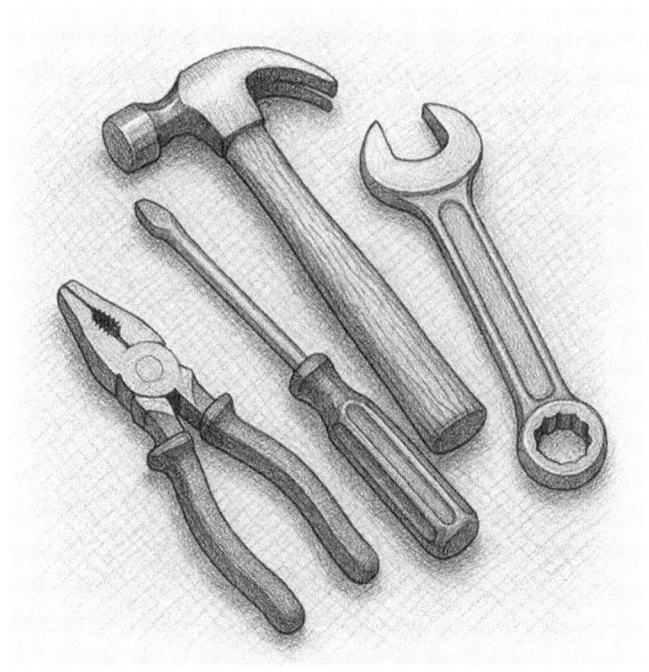

Chapter 5

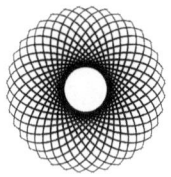

Agile Action

After identifying the gap between your current state and your desired outcome, begin by being vigilant about what you allow your senses to absorb from your surroundings. Craft quality questions to repeatedly reinforce and instil resourcefulness into your subconscious. With the picture now crystal clear in your mind, complement it by creating a vision board that brings a smile to your face every time you look at it. It's time to explore how you can take massive action while being agile during this growth period. Watch the chatter of your inner critic with kindness, and build momentum without losing sight of your goal.

Building Desire

With my goal set in place of aiming to get out of government housing, fuelled with acute desperation, I finally succeeded in purchasing my first home. Up to this point I was bursting with knowledge on properties and maintained momentum after the first purchase. Within a year, I purchased my first investment property, followed by two more in the months after that within my super fund. The desire to leave was so palpable in me that I was determined to keep the momentum going and repeat the process of investing. Reflecting on how I did this, I remember I had asked so many questions to second-tier lenders and real estate agents, that no one could get in the way of the drive I had within me. I found ways to repeat the process over and over, tweaked things along the way and then took blind massive action to achieve my goals.

The things that you have personally wished for so badly **and** achieved in your life mirror the essence of Agile methodologies in businesses and project management. How cool is that? Just as in Agile projects – where teams break down large tasks into manageable steps, prioritise work based on customer value, for example, and adapt plans as needed – you apply similar principles in your personal endeavours. Your ability to identify opportunities, gather information, adapt strategies and take decisive action for that thing you so desire mirrors the Agile approach to project execution. This correlation highlights the universal application and value of strategic approaches not only in business but also in your personal life.

Moreover, relentless pursuit of improvement while growing up and willingness to learn from each experience align with the Agile principle of continuous improvement. Like Agile teams that hold meetings to reflect on past performance and identify areas for enhancement, you embrace a mindset of growth and adaptation, constantly refining your approach to achieve greater success.

Just reiterating that your own personal journey exemplifies the core principles of Agile: flexibility, adaptability and customer (friends and family)-centricity in the conversations you've had over the years. This could be in situations such as a party where you only know a few people, getting your driver's license, going for job interviews and other life experiences. By applying these principles in your personal life, you not only achieve your goals (knowingly or unknowingly) but also demonstrate the transformative power of Agile thinking.

Exercise

In order to experience a high level of agile action, let's create a personal Kanban board. Here's how you do it:

> Find yourself a big board or a nice chunk of wall space. Grab some sticky notes, a bunch of markers (go wild with the colours!) and set up different sections on your board or wall for different focus areas.

> Think about what's important to you at home – money stuff, chores, personal growth, health, family matters – whatever it is, make a section for it. Or you could start with the areas on the health wheel, and as you get familiar with the process, you can change the topics to work on. Some people just have headings such as *Ready, Doing, Done* or *To Do, Next, Doing, Done.*

Once you've got your sections sorted, start jotting down your to-dos on those sticky notes. Keep it simple and clear so you know exactly what needs doing.

Now, stick those notes in their respective sections, but make sure the most urgent ones are up top. That way, you know what to tackle first.

As you start identifying things to do and knocking things off your list, move those sticky notes across your board or wall to the appropriate column (To Do, Next, Doing, Done). Start on the left and work your way to the right as you get stuff done.

Don't forget to check in with your board once a week. Take a look at what you've accomplished, what's still waiting and what new things have popped up. Adjust your priorities if you need to.

By implementing a personal Kanban board, you can get easy jobs done fast and break down complex tasks into manageable steps, prioritise actions and maintain a high level of agility in responding to changes.

Before you know it, you'll be tackling even trickier goals and completing them effortlessly. Breaking down your goals into manageable tasks and physically seeing those action steps in front of you rather than just in your mind clear out all those lingering thoughts that live rent-free in your mind.

Staying agile means being flexible and adapting to different situations and projects as they shift. It's like being a quick problem-solver. By trying out different ways of working, you can find what works best for each situation you face.

It's like finding the right tool for the job. This flexibility helps you work efficiently and get things done faster and smoother.

Frequency

Now that you've become conscious of your thoughts and behaviours and have begun to acknowledge, even if just slightly, the frequency you emit into the space around you, you've taken a significant step forward. I'm genuinely thrilled for you!

Embracing agile action entails freeing oneself from rigid structures and occasionally embracing uncertainty. This openness to relinquishing control and having faith in the unfolding process can result in the release of energetic blockages and resistance, enabling the body to resonate at a more harmonious frequency. You might observe a general increase in vitality and a deepening alignment with your authentic self. This attuning to serene frequencies creates coherence and a deeper connection with the world around us.

Until this point I've written about the concept of vibrational frequency, referring to how fast your body cells move or vibrate. When cells vibrate quickly, they're full of energy and in great shape, which reflects how healthy we feel overall. A healthy human body typically vibrates at a frequency between 62 to 70 million times per second.

Now, when the frequency of our cells drops below 62 million vibrations per second, they can start to change or mutate, leading to illness. Here are some examples:

- When you have a cold or the flu, your body's frequency drops to around 58 million vibrations per second.

- If you have candida in your body, your frequency drops to 55 million vibrations per second.

- With glandular fever (Epstein-Barr virus), your frequency drops to 52 million vibrations per second.

- In the case of cancer, your vibrational frequency drops to 42 million vibrations per second or even lower.

We've explored how our internal thoughts and behaviours affect the frequency we emit. Let's now look at how external factors, such as sound, can also influence our well-being. Just as our internal frequency can impact our health, external sounds can have a profound effect on our cellular vitality.

Studies, like the one published in the Journal of Alternative and Complementary Medicine in 2002, have shown that different frequencies of sound waves can directly affect the structure and function of human cells. For instance, higher-frequency sounds have been found to increase cellular vitality and metabolic activity, while lower-frequency sounds may lead to decreased vitality and altered function. This suggests that certain sounds, like those produced by bells, gongs or crystal bowls, can have a healing effect on the cells of the body, aligning with the concept of vibrational frequency as a key factor in overall health and well-being.

After you've set your sights on your goals, visualised your success and built your vision board, you're now in full

AGILE ACTION

pursuit of what you want. You're running tirelessly toward your dream, with focus razor-sharp and unwavering. Every muscle, every step – precise and intentional. Your eyes stay fixed on the prize. That's you now – moving with purpose, agility and absolute clarity. You're not just dreaming; you're charging forward and staying true to your path, no matter how long it takes.

Keep your focus, stay on course and let nothing stop you! Every movement you make is calculated, every decision aligned with your goal. You're not distracted, you're not hesitating; you're moving with the kind of focus that doesn't waver, no matter the obstacles ahead.

Keep your focus, stay on course and let nothing stop you!

Chapter 6

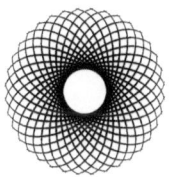

Magnetic Momentum

Hopefully, by now you're getting a little perturbed and a shift has happened in your perspective, mindset and belief systems so that you are a touch uncomfortable. This shift happening with the, perhaps, 'new' information is booting out the old paradigms, which represent all the existing beliefs or programs currently in the driver's seat. It's great to put yourself in uncomfortable situations with awareness!

Brian Tracy, author of Eat That Frog!, advises his high-end clients when hiring for their organisation that if the potential candidate doesn't have at least 20 written goals, they may not be worth hiring. How can you reach your next best self if you haven't even defined the gap? Success leaves clues, and goal setting is one of them. If you're not clear on where you're headed, then how can you expect to get there?

Just like a magnet attracts and repels at opposite ends, your body operates on an energetic frequency, constantly pulling in experiences, people and opportunities that match your internal state. Every thought you think, every belief you hold and every emotion you feel sends out a vibrational signal, shaping your reality. If you want to shift your external world, it starts with tuning your internal magnet to align with your desires.

Remember the high school science experiment with iron filings and a magnet? The iron filings are scattered randomly on a piece of paper. The moment the magnet is placed underneath the paper, the filings arrange themselves to reveal the invisible magnetic field at work. Your body functions in a remarkably similar way – emitting an unseen yet powerful energy field.

If your body is constantly attracting and repelling based on its energetic charge, then understanding what's directing this force becomes crucial.

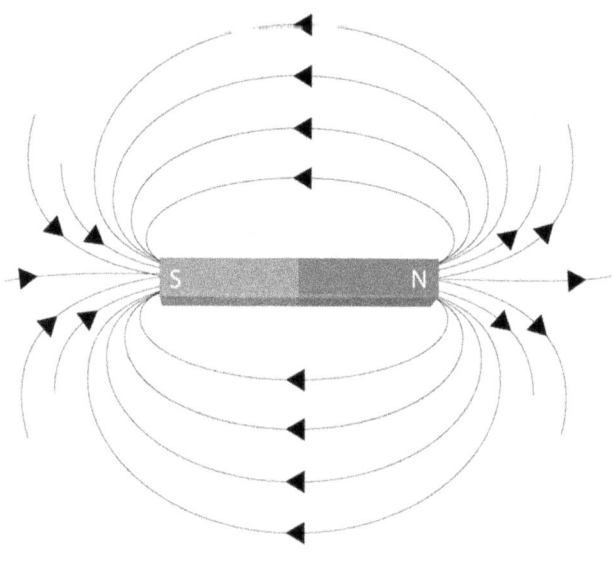

Understanding Paradigms

In our everyday lives, paradigms act as **mental programs** that largely dictate our habitual behaviours, shaping how we perceive, perform and play in the world. While it may seem like these paradigms have exclusive control over our actions, it's important to recognise that we do have the power to consciously intervene and change them.

However, because these paradigms are deeply ingrained through our upbringing, culture and experiences, they often operate unconsciously, influencing our behaviour without us even being aware of the mechanics at play. This is where the power of conscious awareness comes in. By becoming aware of our paradigms or programs and actively working to change them, we can regain control over our actions and ultimately reshape our lives.

Identify the Aspects of Your Life Where Your Paradigm Operates on Autopilot

A paradigm is like the operating system of your mind, similar to Windows or macOS. It runs quietly in the background, influencing how you think and act. This mental software is mostly programmed between ages 0 and 7, when we are learning about our environment and our place in it.

Like outdated software, our paradigm may not meet our current needs. It affects how we view earning money, interpreting events, and managing time, creativity and productivity. Without conscious effort, this programming doesn't update itself and stays in old patterns. Until we choose to upgrade by being present and aware, this system limits our perception of what's possible.

Changing Paradigms

When we identify and decide to change aspects of our life, the mere act of making that decision reduces resistance. Just like the double slit experiment and the fact that when we observe a thought, it doesn't play havoc and take over your thinking for hours. This doesn't mean we've changed anything yet, but it prevents us from hitting a wall so that we know we're on to this and we're going to create momentum.

Examples of Paradigms Passed Down through Generations

Here are two examples of how paradigms can be passed down through generations without questioning why we do things:

Lamb Roast

A young woman named Sue was getting ready to cook a lamb roast for dinner. As she was prepping the lamb, she automatically chopped off the end of the roast. Emily, her daughter, watched curiously and asked, 'Mum, why do you always chop off the end of the lamb roast before cooking it?'

Sue pondered for a moment before responding, 'Well, I'm not exactly sure. That's just how my mum used to do it, so I've always followed her.'

Intrigued by this practice, Emily paid a visit to her grandmother's house and posed the same question. 'Grandma, why do you cut off the end of the lamb roast before cooking it?'

Her grandmother chuckled and replied, 'Oh, that's quite the story. You see, back in the day, my oven was too small to fit the whole roast, so I had to trim it down to make it fit!'

Upon hearing this amusing revelation, Emily shared the story with Sue. They both shared a laugh and decided to put an end to the unnecessary tradition. From then on, they roasted their lamb without cutting off the end, knowing there was no need for such a practice.

Horseradish

John and Angela got married, and as they were getting to know each other a little better, they discovered something amusing about Angela's kitchen habits. Whenever they brought horseradish home from the farmers' market, Angela would only cook the greens and throw away the root.

John found it odd because his family always ate the root and fed the greens to the horses. Angela joked with John, saying 'Who actually eats horseradish roots? We used to give those to the horses!' to which John retorted, 'And who eats the tops? They're incredibly bitter. We give them to the horses!'

Eventually, John and Angela decided to settle the matter by preparing a meal using both the greens and the roots. They realised that each family's traditions had been passed down and adopted as their own. Finally, they found harmony in their kitchen.

Unquestioned Paradigms

Unquestioned paradigms can either be passed down or unchallenged beliefs. People often follow certain behaviours or traditions without understanding the original reason behind them simply because they've always been done that way. It's only when someone stops to question and challenge ways of doing things that they can break free from the mundane and create new, more efficient ways of approaching things.

Contemplation

- **Making money:** Think about how your mindset affects how much money you make. Do you believe you can earn a lot of money, or do you feel like you're always struggling financially?
- **Seeing the world:** Consider how you view or perceive the world around you. Are you generally positive or negative? Do you focus on the good things or the bad things?
- **Time management:** Look at how you use your time. Are you good at getting things done, or do you feel like you're always running out of time?
- **Being creative:** Think about how creative you are. Are you open to new ideas and experiences, or do you stick to what you know?
- **Getting stuff done:** Consider how effective you are at reaching your goals. Do you take action and get things done, or do you procrastinate and put things off?
- **Being productive:** Look at how much you accomplish in a day. Do you feel like you're always busy but not really getting anywhere?

- **Thinking clearly:** Lastly, think about how you make decisions. Do you logically think things through, or do you rely on your feelings?

By examining these areas of your life without preconceived notions and an open mind, you can gain valuable insights into how your underlying beliefs and assumptions influence and impact your behaviour, mindset and overall quality of life. Ask questions to yourself to get to the root of how the thought came in to your consciousness (program).

Questions can halt a program on autopilot. This awareness is key and can serve as a catalyst for personal growth and transformation as you work to adjust your perspective and vibrationally align with your new goals.

The Power of Change – Unlocking Your Next Level

I'd like you to imagine for a moment how much your life will change as you begin improving any or all of the areas above. It will create a massive shift and it will be permanent, because once you invest time and effort to make changes consciously, there's no going back to the old person you were.

Breaking The Cycle – From Past Choices to Future Change

It doesn't matter how hard you work or how many hours you put in. If the underlying paradigm does not change, the results will ultimately remain the same from one year to the next. No point in blaming anything outside of you, especially as an adult. It's past choices that have brought you to where you are now. Think about it: the coffee table in front of you was a choice in the past. The career you're in was a choice in the past. The clothes that you wear on you right now was a purchase choice from a shop you can trace back in the past. Now, what choices will you make today that will take you to a future you love?!

Can I Create a Vibration That Shapes My Destiny?

Absolutely! Just like a phone connects and you can communicate with someone on the other side of the world through a specific frequency, you too can align yourself with the frequency of your goals, not using the outdated program that was on autopilot. The power lies in your ability to manifest your desires into reality.

At present, while your paradigms may currently dictate your vibrations, you possess the inherent capability to shift these vibrations and mould your paradigm to match the reality you wish to create. Everything you seek also has its own frequency. You just have to merge and become one with it. It's a matter of tapping into your innate potential and harnessing the energy within you to manifest your dreams into tangible form.

EVERYTHING YOU WISH FOR ALSO WISHES TO BELONG TO YOU!

> **Side note:** Be sure not to keep chopping and changing too often. Be firm in your decisions and steady in your focus.

Shifting Your Frequency, Shifting Your Life

To move to a much higher frequency of thought, you must first consent and then adapt to the ideas and feelings the new frequency represents. See the new image of you achieving your goal in your mind's eye, and fuel it with feelings to change your vibrations. This is not an easy thing to uphold, as your old circumstances will still be all around you. They are in harmony with your old paradigm, but you consciously made a decision that that is not going to control you anymore. So let me tell you, if I can do it in the circumstances that I was in, you surely can do it.

Momentum in Motion

Jump over the fence from knowledge to experiencing it firsthand by taking action. You can only attract what you are in harmony with. Energy attracts like energy. The beauty of experience is that once you've attracted one goal into your life, you **know** you can do it again. Experience tells you; you know you can!

The Physical Heart and Its Invisible Power Grid

The heart, a vortex that pumps blood to all parts of your body through the circulatory system, works with a network of arteries, veins and capillaries, delivering oxygen, nutrients, hormones and waste products to the right areas with precision to support cells and keep them healthy, actively exchanging and flowing, depending on the quality of the foods we eat. While the heart physically pumps blood to sustain life, it simultaneously processes and circulates thought forms energetically, influencing the vibrational field that surrounds and connects us through connecting and interconnecting threads.

Going back to the energetic toroidal field, the heart generates the largest electromagnetic field surrounding the body, constantly churning data from our environment and processing it – throwing out what it doesn't need and keeping what it finds useful. As there is already a cycle of flow happening, it's time to be a little choosy about what you let into your field and what you discard, becoming aware of the vibrational frequency that you are resonating with or giving out.

Beyond its physical function, the heart also has an energetic or electric component, expanding the thoughts from your thinking and spreading them into the atmosphere.

Have you ever walked into a room full of people and felt the tension or joy without a word being spoken? That's your heart tuning in to the broadcast of the space. It's the unconscious intelligence within you, finding the people radiating at the same frequency that you are radiating. The extension of your energetic field overlaps with theirs, and you almost instantly get a 'match' resonance, indication or a message to talk to or not to approach a certain person – all automatically done within a couple of seconds. Very intelligent.

Dynamic Intersection Point – Where the Physical, Mental and Energetic Meet

Imagine yourself standing in the eye of a storm. Around you, the winds howl, the rain lashes and chaos churns. But in the centre, where you stand, there is stillness. Each element – the wind, the rain, the thunder – belongs to its own domain, doing what it is meant to do. They swirl and interact, yet they never touch the calm at the core.

This stillness represents the dynamic intersection – a space within you where the physical, mental and energetic realms converge. The storm symbolises life's essential forces – the physical winds carrying the weight of your body and its needs, the mental rain showering you with both deliberate and uncontrolled thoughts, and the thunder of energy pulsing outward, radiating your presence into the world. Yet, in the eye of the storm, all this activity revolves around your ability to remain steady, observing and harmonising these elements while rooted in calm.

The Transformational Gateway – Bridging the Seen and Unseen

This dynamic intersection point is a transformational gateway – a living connection between the tangible processes of your body, the intangible patterns of your mind and the expansive energy field that connects you to the greater world. It is the centre of your being, where the physical (what you consume and how it nourishes you), the mental (your thoughts and emotions) and the energetic (the vibrations you emit) converge and shape your reality.

At this gateway, every choice you make in your physical and mental realms ripples outward into the expansive energy field surrounding you, referred to as the toroidal field. The heart, as the epicentre of this field, plays a pivotal role by generating an electromagnetic force that bridges your internal and external worlds. Whether you are aware of it or not, this energy interacts with your environment, influencing your personal experience and your contribution to the collective atmosphere.

A Tool for Quantum Shifts

When approached with awareness, this space becomes a tool for transformation. Aligning what you feed your body, the thoughts you entertain and the emotions you allow to surface creates a harmonious resonance within you. This resonance determines the vibrational frequency you project, turning your energetic field into a reflection of intentional living. The more conscious you are of this process, the greater your ability to influence your reality and the energy you contribute to the world.

The Heart: Your Personal Radio Station

Research from the HeartMath Institute tells us that the heart generates a powerful electromagnetic field extending up to 3 feet from the body. However, it's not just 3 feet. That's the extent of the measuring devices' capabilities! It extends out and goes on forever! Like a radio station, it broadcasts, transmits and receives signals, influencing our surroundings.

The Four Dynamic Forces of the Heart:

1. **Broadcasting Signals**: The heart's electromagnetic field acts like a broadcast tower, influencing your physical body and the energy you exchange with others.
2. **Transmitting Information**: The heart sends emotional and electrical signals into your surroundings, synchronised with your emotional state.

3. **Reception and Transmission**: Just like a radio receiver, the heart picks up external frequencies from others, creating an energetic exchange.
4. **Tuning Frequencies**: The heart tunes into emotional frequencies – whether love, gratitude or stress – like selecting a station on the radio.

What Are You Broadcasting?

The frequencies you emit influence how others perceive and respond to you. If you fill yourself with gratitude – what Abraham Hicks calls a Rampage of Appreciation – you flood your energy field with positive vibrations that resonate for hours. Conversely, if you allow negative thoughts to spiral, your energy field reflects that, often leading to feelings of heaviness or depression.

The Rampage of Appreciation technique emphasises shifting focus to positive aspects of life to elevate the emotional state. Esther and Jerry Hicks, through their Abraham-Hicks YouTube channel, offer teachings on the law of attraction and manifestation.[9]

'Hey Mr DJ, Can You Play That Song?'

You are the DJ of your heart's radio station, choosing the music of your emotions, thoughts and energy. By consciously tuning into higher emotional states, you set the frequency that builds magnetic momentum, attracting experiences and opportunities that align with your energy.

Priming Your Vibrational Frequency

By understanding and aligning with your vibrational frequency, you can accelerate the manifestation of your desires. Through daily practices like reading your list of goals or visualising your vision board, your intentions enter your awareness, making it easier to act on opportunities aligned with them.

Releasing Old Habits and Patterns

As you cultivate new frequencies, be ready to release old patterns and habits that no longer serve you. By mastering your energy field, you step into your power, transforming not only your inner world but also your connection to the collective atmosphere. Your journey toward alignment and intentional creation has just begun.

Exercise

The Ultimate Sonic Purge Recalibration

1. **Submerge and Breathe**: Immerse yourself in a warm bath with Epsom or rock salts, close your eyes and take a slow, deep breath. Hold briefly, then exhale slowly. Repeat five to ten times, allowing the water and breath to ground you and activate the magnetic momentum within.
2. **Hum and Vibrate**: Hum a resonant "Hmmm" with your tongue against the roof of your mouth. Start low and gradually raise the pitch. Let the vibrations fill your chest, throat and head, building momentum for 10 minutes or as long as it feels good.

3. **Sonic Purge Release**: Take a deep, cleansing breath, feeling the vibrations clear any stagnation. Let the energy recalibrate and move through you, amplifying the magnetic pull of your inner core, grounding and revitalising you with each breath. Vigorously shake it off!

Chapter 7

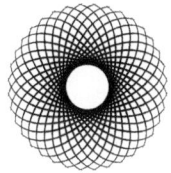

Make Magic

There is a quiet wonder to the creative process. It begins with a spark of intention – a wish, a vision – and transforms it into something real. For centuries, this process has been cloaked in words like *magic*, yet its essence is no mystery. A slight of hand that a magician has practised for thousands of hours is not magic! It's calculated and repeated over and over till it's smooth and seamless.

Bridging the gap is a deliberate act of aligning your inner wishes with the infinite possibilities of realising them in the outer world.

When was the last time you felt truly aligned? Was there a moment when everything you did felt effortless, as if the universe had conspired to open portals of possibilities just for you? That is the essence of magic – alignment!

The Feeling of Alignment

Alignment is the harmony or resonance between belief, intention and action. When you are aligned, opportunities seem to appear out of nowhere. However, this is not random. It's the result of your energy matching the frequency of what you desire. It's your hard inner work made manifest.

Alignment begins with clarity. Clarity is where the magic lies.

Back in the day, radio transmitters required careful tuning to pick up stations clearly. If you were even slightly off, static interference disrupted the signal and you couldn't hear the broadcast of your favourite music. Similarly, your goals and desires operate on unique frequencies. To bring them to fruition, you must align yourself with their energy your thoughts, feelings and actions acting as the tuning dials.

If you're perfectly tuned in, you'll feel in sync and attract opportunities effortlessly, like being at the right place at the right time. But if you're slightly off, doubts, fears or distractions – your internal static – may disrupt the connection.

Finding alignment begins with clarity – a precise understanding of your goals. When you take the time to define what you truly wish for, whether by writing it down, speaking it aloud or simply allowing it to fill your mind, you set the foundation for transformation. From there, your energy begins to shape your vibration, drawing opportunities that resonate with your confidence, joy and gratitude.

Achieving alignment requires patience and intention. Craft statements that reflect your desires, words you can repeat daily to anchor your focus. As you eliminate the static of doubt and negativity, your attention sharpens on what you're aiming for, and the path ahead begins to unfold with greater clarity.

The Power of Words

Every word you speak shapes your reality. They carry a vibration and intention. The ancient phrase *abracadabra*, 'I create as I speak', is more than a magical chant or a spell before a magician waves his wand; it's a reminder of the important connection between what we speak (language) and what we create.

Words are seeds. Speak doubt and fear, and you will have obstacles; speak expansion and determination, and they blossom into possibility.

What stories do you repeat over and over to your friends and to yourself about your days? Casual comments like 'I'm so stressed', 'I'll never be able to do that', 'I'll never get it right', 'I'm always behind' are spells repeated often enough to become truths.

Turn that around to speak words of power: 'I am fully capable of completing this', 'I am worthy', 'I am learning to navigate my days with grace', 'I am on the path to my grand future'. Statements like these unlock possibilities and bridge the gap to what you wish to see in your world.

Rituals and the Role of Repetition

Magic is a practice that's repeated, crafted, tweaked and refined so that the performance is seamless to the audience.

For your intentions to be embedded into the fabric of your subconscious, engage all of your sensory organs as much as possible to override the current, lifelong and, perhaps, stubborn programmes of your mind by doing the following daily:

1. Write it down. Do something tactile.
2. Read it out aloud. Voice is a vibration much like a portal bringing something into creation.
3. Read it silently.
4. Visualise a clear mental picture of yourself in the environment as having achieved your goal.

The act of repetition anchors you, turning priming thoughts into unshakable beliefs and emanating vibrations of gratitude of having your wish already in your life! This daily ritual becomes second nature over time, hopefully to the point that you can't go a day without priming.

Injecting the manual programming invites synchronicity into your life. To keep this up is the hardest part, as there are no tangible results to immediately see around you. So, it requires a little effort at the start to make it second nature.

Shifting Energy through Challenges

Since your default mode of past programming is a strong force and the easiest path of least resistance, with this daily ritual the mind will try to protect and defend itself from the new, often clinging to the old stories and justifying lack and limitation – the familiar way that it's used to!

Rewrite the stories and permanently override your past programming!

When fear (old programs) whispers 'I'm not enough', respond with a spell of resilience and nurture, 'I am learning and growing in a new way'.

Each repetition strengthens the new program and replaces the old, which is the goal.

Magic in Everyday Life

A mere mortal's magic doesn't demand grand gestures. It thrives in the mundane. It's in the morning rituals of gratitude with what you already have, the pause at midday to realign your centre and the quiet moments before bed when you speak your wishes into being. These practices are programming the change you wish to see in your future as you become the co-creator.

Humble–Quiet–Steady

When you approach life with intention and repetition, you become the architect of your reality. Magic, then, is not a distant force; it is the powerful energy force being harnessed within you. Once you're in harmony with your goals, they'll seem to flow naturally toward you, as if the universe itself is conspiring in your favour.

My First City2Surf Race

The Challenge

There was a time when running even a few kilometres felt like a monumental task. I had always admired those who could complete long-distance races, but the thought of attempting something like the City2Surf – a 14-kilometre run – seemed out of reach. My friend, seeing something in me that I didn't yet see in myself, encouraged me to enter. At first, I hesitated. Was I really cut out for this? I was far from an experienced runner. But why not try? So, with a mix of curiosity and determination, I signed up to the 'back of the pack' blue bib and all, ready to see how far I could push myself.

This wasn't just about running; it was about proving to myself that I could take on a challenge that felt bigger than me. I decided to focus on the journey rather than the outcome.

The Process

I started small. Each morning, I laced up my shoes and went for a run, no matter how short. At first, it was tough – my legs ached, my breathing was laboured, and my mind would come up with every excuse to stop. But I kept at it.

Slowly, I built a ritual – visualising myself crossing the finish line, repeating affirmations like 'I am strong, I am capable' and focusing on each step rather than the distance ahead. I started training daily. The first few runs were humbling – short distances leave me out of breath, and I'd catch myself questioning if I could even complete the race. But my friend's belief in me, paired with my growing resolve, kept me going.

I also began to imagine the energy of the race day – all the other runners, the cheers of the crowd, the sense of accomplishment waiting at the finish line, the feeling of doing something I'd never done before. I repeated the affirmations: 'I can do this easily', 'One step at a time', 'I'm stronger than I think'.

Over time, my endurance grew and so did my confidence. These mental images and the words I repeated over and over became my anchor, helping me push through the days when progress felt slow.

The Breakthrough

When race day finally arrived, I was nervous but determined. The energy in the air was electric. Standing at the starting line, surrounded by thousands of runners, I felt both nervous and exhilarated. I watched people do warm up exercises, so instead of waiting for the start gun, I copied what others around me were doing without making it obvious.

As the race began, I focused on my breath, my stride and the rhythm of my steps. The first few kilometres flew by, the middle stretch tested my endurance. By the time I reached Heartbreak Hill, my legs ached, but my heart pushed me forward. I was determined not to stop. Every step felt like a triumph over the doubts I had carried into this journey.

As I neared the finish line, I was greeted by the sound of cheers. Strangers lined the sidelines, clapping and shouting words of encouragement. It wasn't until later that I realised their enthusiasm was partly because I was one of the few blue-bib runners coming through from the back of the pack. But in that moment, I wasn't running for anyone else. I was running for me.

Crossing that finish line wasn't just the end of a race; it was the start of a new understanding and proof of what I could achieve when I aligned my intention, effort and belief.

The Reflection

Since that day, I've run 15 City2Surfs. Each one has its own story, its own rhythm – but none have been as magical as the first. That first race was about stepping into a version of myself I didn't know existed.

It all started with a friend who believed in me and a decision to take on a challenge that felt beyond my reach. That race became a reminder that magic happens when you align with your vision, commit to the process, **take action** and dare to believe in what's possible.

Chapter 8

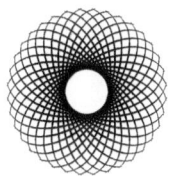

Present Peace

The present moment is inevitable. It holds everything – the warm, lovely moments of childhood, the unfinished loops in the psyche from yesterday's 'what could have been' and the imagined threats and worries of tomorrow.[10]

When you relax into the present – perhaps through meditation – it stops feeling like a struggle and opens to a vast stillness that so many of us yearn for. Yet, for many, the offer of peace from the present feels just out of reach, overshadowed by the endless chatter of the mind.

When we pause long enough to feel the vast present, something extraordinary happens. The weight of striving begins to lift, the noise quiets, and a stillness that was always there begins to emerge. The world outside doesn't change, but our relationship to it softens. In this moment, with all its imperfections, there is a sense of enoughness. It emerges in awareness – the subtle recognition of the breath you didn't realise you were holding, the way the light falls on certain objects in the room you're in, the feeling of the texture of clothes against your skin – the simple act of noticing. You don't want to force life anymore. You want to flow and bask in it.

Through this lens, challenges begin to look different. They lose their sharp edge, becoming part of the unfolding story rather than obstacles in the way. From this place of stillness, clarity rises – not from overthinking or striving, but from allowing life to unfold moment by moment.

Settle into this energy, frequency and vibration, the dynamic forces that are already happening from your blood flow and electricity in your cells and life force energy from birth till now.

Connect and bring this thread of stillness forward to feel strong and be the predominant creative force in your life. Start by taking care of yourself emotionally. Fill your own cup with gratefulness until it overflows. When we're emotionally fulfilled, we automatically spread that gratitude and positivity to those around us.

Measuring progress and improving every step of the way is the most rewarding journey. As we focus on our own inner peace, our trust in ourselves builds and we also become better equipped to handle life's challenges with strength and authenticity.

To get closer to having peace and calm within us in each present moment, think of our bodies as both batteries, which store energy chemically, and capacitors, which store energy electrically. Both are devices designed to store and release energy. Batteries function because of the electrolyte salts inside them, allowing the flow of energy, using liquid salts to regulate and enhance the batteries.

Bodies as batteries: Our bodies have a finite potential. We accumulate energy through sources such as food, sunlight and experiences (mentally), much like a battery storing chemical energy.

Just as batteries gradually lose their efficiency over time with repeated charging and discharging cycles, our bodies may experience fatigue and decreased energy levels with prolonged exertion or stress.

Capacitor as energetic field: Conversely, our bodies can also act as capacitors, which store and release electrical energy in an electric field and control the flow of energy better. In this analogy, our energetic field encompasses not only physical energy but also emotional, mental and spiritual elements intertwined.

So, it's important to treat our bodies well to keep our inner peace. With regular practices like meditation, daily priming and self-care, our energy can stay strong and adaptable over time. Stress builds up in the body and needs a daily drain out!

While vitamins are often praised for keeping us healthy, minerals are the real heroes. Giving our bodies the right minerals – including the tissue cell salts that align with what our body needs – helps balance our body's electrical energy and keeps the energetic crossover flow between the two channels open, ensuring restoration is uninterrupted and everything flows smoothly.

When the right minerals, particularly the tissue salts tailored to our needs, are running through our system, the connectivity of finer tissues within is enhanced, and the energetic body becomes vibrant and clear. These minerals create strong pathways from the physical to the energetic, nourishing our emotional body. As a result, we'll overthrow lower vibrational states such as depression, sadness, melancholy and inactivity, as they no longer serve us.

By taking care of your body physically, energetically and with the right minerals, you can find peace and harmony within yourself, equipping you to handle life's challenges with strength and grace.

We Are Made from the Fundamental Salt of the Earth

Our bodies, like the earth itself, are composed of essential elements that support balance, vitality and overall well-being. Just as minerals shape the physical world, they also play a fundamental role in maintaining our internal harmony.

Anyone who knows me well knows that I use salt as a remedy for everything – from cleaning to bathing, from space clearing to health – knowing that salt heals all. It's a powerful and natural purifier, both physically and energetically, making it an essential tool for restoring balance in many aspects of life.

To support the body's natural equilibrium and maintain vibrant energy, the 12 tissue salts are an excellent tool. Below is a simple table to help you understand and choose the right salts based on your needs. Consider these salts a key element in bridging the gap between physical wellness and inner peace.

Category	Tissue Salt	Key Benefits	Quick Hint
Calcium (Strength)	Calc Fluor (Calcium Fluoride)	Elasticity, connective tissues, teeth	Flexibility and firmness
	Calc Phos (Calcium Phosphate)	Bone growth, repair, energy	Strong bones and vitality
	Calc Sulph (Calcium Sulphate)	Skin healing, detoxification	Clears skin and wounds
Iron (Oxygenation)	Ferr Phos (Iron Phosphate)	Oxygen transport, inflammation reduction	First aid for energy and relief
Potassium (Balance)	Kali Mur (Potassium Chloride)	Mucous health, digestion	Clears congestion and mucus
	Kali Phos (Potassium Phosphate)	Nervous system, stress relief	Peaceful nerves and clarity
	Kali Sulph (Potassium Sulphate)	Detox, skin and cell renewal	Skin glow and cellular cleansing
Magnesium (Calm)	Mag Phos (Magnesium Phosphate)	Muscle cramps, nerve relaxation	Relax muscles and mind
Sodium (Hydration)	Nat Mur (Sodium Chloride)	Water balance, emotional stability	Hydrates body and emotions
	Nat Phos (Sodium Phosphate)	Acidity balance, digestion	Neutralises acid, aids digestion
	Nat Sulph (Sodium Sulphate)	Liver detox, water regulation	Detoxes liver and drains excess
Silica (Resilience)	Silica (Dioxide)	Cleansing, hair, skin, nails	Strengthens beauty and resilience

The 12 Tissue Salts: A Quick Reference for Balancing Body and Mind

> **Important Note:** The information provided in this book, including the tissue salts table, is intended for general knowledge and personal exploration. While tissue salts are widely regarded as a gentle and supportive approach to well-being, it's always best to listen to your body and seek advice from a qualified healthcare professional or naturopath, especially if you have any existing health conditions, are pregnant or are taking other medications.

Your journey to balance and vitality is unique; consulting a professional ensures you're making choices that align with your specific needs and goals.

Salt: A Conduit for Renewal

If you're ready to let go of thoughts or bits of your identity about being 'right' or feelings that are not serving you – like anger, sadness, shame, fear and guilt – then this process of purging daily and surrendering to achieve present peace can happen much sooner than waiting until your deathbed! This may sound a little harsh; however, thoughts are really things, and they stick! They stick around in your energetic field in the form of positive ions, sometimes for days! Stress and fatigue can also lead to the creation of positive ions, which have a positive electrical charge. This can build up throughout the day, weighing you down and affecting your mood.

Beyond its physical health benefits, salt is a natural amplifier of energy. It has long been revered as a toll for purification, washing away stagnant heaviness and restoring balance.

To start a daily purging process, do one of the following daily:

- Rigorous exercise by joining a gym, running or swimming. Rigorous exercise speeds up the flow of the toroidal fields in and around the body, activated by the automatic increased breathing and movement.

- Learn a dynamic breathwork technique, such as the Wim Hof Method. Organisations like the Art of Living Foundation and Isha Foundation as well as Joe Dispenza offer courses on unique dynamic breathwork to activate your energy.

- Swim in the ocean year-round. The ocean's hydro energy and sandy shores vibrate at a high frequency, neutralising positive ions in the body. Although the ocean contains both positive and negative ions, natural settings such as the ocean, especially around crashing waves and waterfalls, are renowned for generating a surplus of negative ions. The fastest way to purge your energetic field of the positive ions is to dive into the salty ocean and shock the body.

- Practice the ultimate sonic purge calibration at home, wash yourself with salt or indulge in baths with Epsom salts mixed with equal parts bicarbonate of soda and a cup of apple cider vinegar.

These practices can effectively cleanse the mind, body and spirit so that daily thoughts are dropped, then your body is not bogged down, paving the way for good feelings.

The Heart's Stillness Meditation

Take a moment to find a comfortable seat. Close your eyes and take a deep, slow breath in ... and gently exhale. Feel your body settle as you take another breath in ... and let it out. One more deep breath, allowing calm to wash over you as you exhale fully.

Now, in your mind's eye, imagine yourself seated in a lotus position. See yourself clearly – your body calm, your posture serene. With each breath, you begin to shrink, becoming smaller and smaller, like a tiny figurine, small enough to fit in the palm of your hand.

Feel yourself gently settle into this new, miniature version of you. In this form, your body feels light, pure and unburdened.

As you sit, notice a warm glow in the centre of your chest – a soft, pure white light emanating from your heart. It radiates gently, filling the space around you with a sense of peace and serenity.

Pause. (10 seconds)

Now, feel yourself being softly drawn towards the source of this light. Like a feather floating on a breeze, you drift downward, gliding into the glowing white heart space within you.

Pause. (15 seconds)

You find yourself seated at the very base of your heart, where the rhythmic beats of life surround you. Feel the gentle pulse ... one beat ... then another. Steady. Reassuring. Eternal.

Pause. (15 seconds)

Let yourself merge with this rhythm, each beat guiding you deeper into stillness. With every pulse, feel your awareness expand, stretching outward like ripples on a still pond. You are both small and infinite. Present and timeless.

Pause. (20 seconds)

Notice how the beats of your heart anchor you, keeping you grounded in this vast, peaceful space. Here, nothing else matters. There is no rush, no noise – only the steady pulse of life and the boundless stillness between each beat.

Pause. (30 seconds)

In this space, feel yourself connected to something greater. Each beat is a reminder of your connection to all that is. The stillness between the beats holds infinite possibilities, infinite peace.

Pause. (30 seconds)

Breathe deeply into this moment. Let the glow of your heart expand, surrounding you with warmth and serenity. Each beat is a reminder that peace resides here, always within you.

Pause. (20 seconds)

Now, take a moment to gently return. Feel the pulse of your heart as an anchor, grounding you back to your body. Slowly, see yourself rise, growing back to your original size, bringing with you the calm and stillness of your heart's rhythm.

Pause. (15 seconds)

Take a deep breath in, feeling the peace you've cultivated. Exhale slowly. When you're ready, gently open your eyes, carrying this sense of infinite stillness and calm with you into the rest of your day.

Guidelines for Recording Your Personal Trigger for Peace

Create your space:

Find a quiet, comfortable spot where you feel at ease. Open your voice recorder app and take a moment to settle into a peaceful state before beginning.

Speak with calm intention:

As you read the meditation aloud, let your voice flow naturally, with warmth and softness. Leave gentle pauses where you feel they belong, allowing space for reflection and calm between phrases. Longer pauses work best as they take you deeper into the stillness

Keep it simple and personal:

Once recorded, name it something meaningful, like 'Heart-Centred Peace'. Let this recording be your daily companion, a soothing guide to help you reconnect with your inner stillness.

Part 3
THE GIFT

Chapter 9

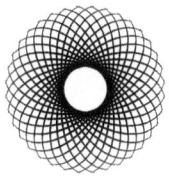

Constant Change

Life is a journey of constant change – an intriguing paradox. Change is the only constant, but it's not change itself that people fear. It's the loss of the familiar. We fear what we don't know – the unknown that can shake the ground beneath us. Sudden change can feel like a punch in the gut, unsettling and jarring. Yet, incremental change, when approached with awareness and communicated in advance, offers the possibility of new opportunities and fresh starts.

I remember the years when life felt like a blur. It was as if I was caught in a whirlwind, constantly being tossed from one place to another. In just two years, I moved nine times. Nine! Every new home felt like a new beginning – new neighbourhoods, new faces, new adventures. But the exhilaration of house hunting, meeting agents and exploring spaces didn't mask

BRIDGE THAT GAP

the deeper truth. Beneath the surface, I was spiralling. My marriage had just ended, I was facing single motherhood, and I had no idea how to hold it all together.

At first, the change felt like chaos. The more things shifted, the more I resisted. But over time, I began to see it differently. I wasn't just moving houses; I was moving through my life, from one phase to the next, one version of myself to the next. Change wasn't happening to me; it was happening *through* me. It was shaping me.

A shift in perspective is a bridge to resilience.

I realised something vital: If I wanted to steer my life in a forward direction, I had to stop running from my past. I had to face it head-on. I had to confront the traumas, the mistakes, the heartbreak. And I had to forgive – myself and others. Each lesson, each experience became the fuel for my transformation. These were the years of my deepest learning.

Just like the shoreline, constantly reshaped by the tide, our lives are in constant flux. The key isn't to fear the waves – it's to ride them. To steer the ship instead of being tossed by the storm. Because as Wayne Dyer wisely said, 'Change the way you look at things, and the things you look at change.'

In those moments of uncertainty, when it felt like the earth was shifting beneath me, I began to **choose** how I responded. Yes, things were changing rapidly, but what if I embraced it? What if I didn't just endure the change but **thrived** on it?

I went from dreading the unknown to seeking it. The first time I stepped into a new house, I was terrified. What was I doing? Where was I going? But the second time? The third time? I felt a thrill. I saw the potential in the blank spaces, the opportunity to create a new warm space for myself and my children.

Life had become a series of open doors – some slammed in my face, some wide open, beckoning me forward. And every time I walked through one of those doors, I felt a little freer and stronger.

But it wasn't just the external changes that transformed me. It was the internal shift. I moved from resistance to acceptance. I stopped fighting the changes around me and started embracing them. I stopped holding on to what was **comfortable** and started moving towards what was **possible**.

Change isn't the enemy. It's the discomfort that comes with change that we fear. The uncertainty. The unknowing. But what I discovered through every move, every setback, every new beginning is that change is **an opportunity**. It's something to be welcomed.

And now, as I face new challenges, new unknowns, I've learned to welcome the shift. The pace of life may be relentless, but it's also exhilarating. Every change, every transition, is an opportunity to grow, to evolve. The question isn't whether change will come; it's whether you're ready to meet it head-on, to *create* the change you want to see in your life. Deliberately making changes to get out of your comfort zone every once in a while keeps you on your toes!

As I look back on the whirlwind of constant change in my life, I now realise how it's been more than just a series of challenges – it's been a gift. At first, it felt like a force beyond my control, a storm that uprooted me time and again. But with each new change, I learned something about myself that I wouldn't have discovered otherwise.

I remember when I was about 6 years old, all the early Saturday mornings when my sister and I were left alone while Mum and Dad went to the markets. At the time, I didn't understand why money seemed so important. Why was it that the very thing that sustained us was also what kept our parents occupied and away from us? As a child, it felt like a loss. But looking back, I now see how money, and the need to work for it, was the first form of change that taught me about resilience, about adaptation and how we must constantly adjust to the forces outside our control. It was an early lesson in embracing the ebb and flow of life's circumstances, even when they didn't seem to align with my desires.

Then there were the rules around relationships, particularly the way my sister and I were discouraged from interacting with boys. This constant separation created an almost unnatural sense of caution, and as I grew older I realised it kept me from forming healthy relationships with the opposite sex. However, instead of viewing this as a limitation, I now see it as a gift that helped me examine my own beliefs about connection and communication. I've come to realise that these early challenges in understanding relationships gave me the space to reframe and redefine what I wanted in my life. The discomfort of this imposed isolation eventually led me to healthier, more authentic ways of connecting with others.

The changing dynamics in my home – where discipline often hinged on the phrase 'Wait till your father gets home' – was another constant change I encountered. As a child, I was confused. Why didn't Mum just handle things on her own? Why did Dad need to be the authority figure? This pushed me to question authority, to think critically about power dynamics and ultimately to carve my own path as a leader. It was through those shifts in power that I learned what it truly meant to take control and step into my own power – something that would become crucial later on in my career.

And then came the workplace. I entered a male-dominated environment where I saw men rise to leadership positions with ease, and I couldn't help but question myself. Were they smarter? Did they know something I didn't? But instead of staying stuck in those questions, I saw it as a challenge that prompted me to rise above my doubts and push through the limits I had unknowingly imposed on myself.

The constant shifts in my environment – both in the workplace and in my home life – kept me from staying stagnant. They forced me to adapt, grow and stretch beyond what I thought was possible. In doing so, I found my own path – someone who could navigate change, support others and lead with compassion and vision.

I see how constant change has always been a gift in disguise. It's in the moments of discomfort, when life pulls us in new directions, that we find the potential to reinvent ourselves. Each change – no matter how jarring – has taught me resilience, flexibility and the ability to see opportunity where others see only loss. I've learned that change is not something to fear or resist, but something to embrace, learn from and grow through.

Change is the gift that keeps on giving, propelling us forward, shaping us into who we are meant to become. The key is to reframe change, from disruption to an opportunity to grow and evolve.

Change is uncomfortable at the early stages of any new venture. It nudges us out of our comfort zones. Old habitual patterns hang around and stay dominant in our behaviour just because we are used to it. So, see it as a gift of growth, and it will propel us forward and leave the emotional baggage behind with good, solid commitment.

Kindly note, if you ever find yourself struggling or in need of support, please reach out to a registered psychologist or mental health professional. They are trained to help navigate through life's challenges and can provide valuable guidance and support along your journey.

Exercise

Reflect on a time when your life experienced sudden change. Write about how you felt in the moment – anxious, excited, fearful or uncertain. Now answer these questions:

- How did you eventually adapt to this change?

- What lessons did you learn from that experience?

- Are you facing any change right now? How can you approach it with excitement, not fear?

- Think of one thing you can do today to embrace a change happening in your life, no matter how small.

Change is inevitable, but growth is optional – because in the end, perspective is everything.

Chapter 10

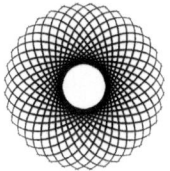

Final Frontier

The phrase 'the final frontier' is usually associated with unexplored areas of a particular domain. The term gained popularity in the opening scenes of the Star Trek series in 1966, spoken by Captain James T Kirk saying, 'Space, the final frontier.', then in the Red Hot Chili Peppers song 'Californication' with the line 'Space may be the final frontier but it's made in a Hollywood basement'.

Scientists presumably understand more about outer space than they do about the brain. There are countless connections in the brain, possibly more than there are stars in the Milky Way. Connecting the dots between outer space and our own thoughts, 'the final frontier' is like saying there's a big unknown out there, but it's not just about outer space, stars and planets; I believe the final frontier is about what's happening in the space between our ears and inside our heads and exploring the depths of our own minds, which are often uncharted territory.

Our thoughts and inner experiences can be as vast and mysterious as the universe itself. Yet, many questions about the brain remain unanswered, such as why we dream or why some people experience cognitive decline with age, while others maintain normal function.

Moving from the big picture to our personal lives, there is a tiny gland located in the centre of the two hemispheres of our brain in the epithalamus. Called the pineal gland, it's shaped like a tiny pinecone and serves as a symbolic representation to understand ourselves better. While relatively small, the pineal gland has important functions, including the secretion of melatonin – a hormone that regulates the sleep–wake cycle or circadian rhythms of our body.

Furthermore, the pineal gland has been associated with serving as a connection between the physical world, spiritual beliefs and metaphysical concepts. Casually referred to as the biological 'third eye' in certain cultures, the pineal gland symbolises its association with our higher consciousness.

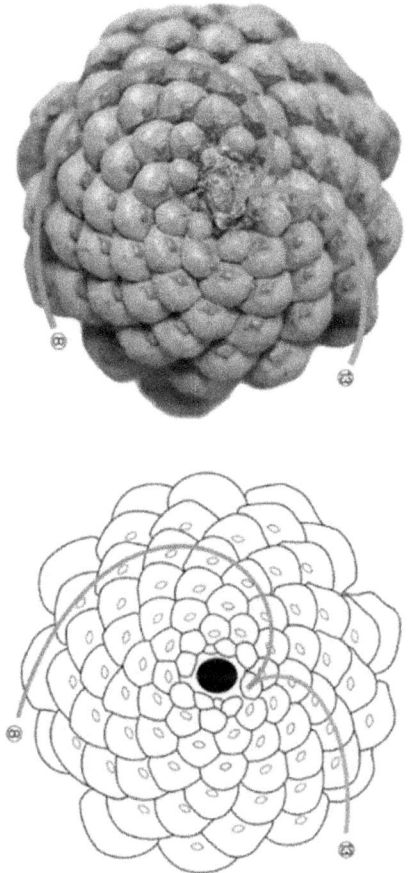

I personally see the shape of the pineal gland as an indicator that we are constantly expanding as individuals, presenting an opportunity to keep improving throughout our time on Earth. If you explore the history books of different cultures around the world, you will find the pinecone depicted in several places – on the end of statues holding a staff, in family crests, in front of large corporate buildings, and in ancient and modern religions, among many other areas – always symbolising growth.

Beyond the Puppet: Pinocchio's Hidden Meaning

Are you familiar with the classic tale of Pinocchio? Pinocchio is a wooden puppet that has been carved by Geppetto. The puppet comes to life and starts speaking. He realises that when he is not true to his own nature, his wooden nose grows, and it becomes very uncomfortable. When we look at how Pinocchio evolves and learns about himself, it's like a mirror to our own journey of figuring out who we are.

The word *Pinocchio* can be broken down into two words: *Pin*, resembling *pine*, and *Occhio*, which translates to *eye* in Italian. Therefore, the name Pinocchio symbolises the single eye in the middle of our head or the pineal gland.

Pinocchio is on a quest for freedom and change, much like we're all trying to find our place in life. Recognising that Pinocchio is a puppet, we interpret his plight to become a real person as an allegory for achieving the things we desire in our lives by ascending one level up from where we are by activating our pineal gland.

Imagine the blue fairy in Pinocchio as your spiritual coach, nudging you to wake up. She whispers, 'You have free choice; however, let me introduce you to some cool stuff like meditation and practising stillness so that you give out good vibes.' She guides you towards being better and better, gently reminding you of the power within to transform your reality and get more of what you wish for in life.

Jiminy Cricket serves as Pinocchio's external conscience, a guide and moral compass who advocates honesty, bravery and taking responsibility. There will always be temptations leading you astray along the journey to your desired outcome.

Additionally, Jiminy Cricket represents the internal aspect of our psyche known as the superego, embodying the voice of morality and ethical decision-making within us.

This activation to give out good vibes requires commitment, avoiding self-deception and resisting external influences that don't serve us. Avoiding stimulants like caffeine and heavily processed foods, like sugar and flour, helps keep your pineal gland clean, lessen brain fog and clear your thinking.

In essence, the story of Pinocchio serves as a metaphorical guide to achieving authenticity in our daily lives. As Pinocchio stumbles and falls and sorts out the dramas in his life, he eventually succeeds in becoming a real, live boy. The same goes for us. If we drop the unnecessary things in our lives and live a simple, clean life, we activate our 'Pinocchio' – our pineal gland – and are on our way to getting crystal clear in what we wish to see in our lives, finding inner comfort and ready to unleash that inner magic!

The Impact of Words, Thoughts and Emotions

Words

As I discussed in Chapter 3: 'Quality Questions', the words we use have a certain resonance long after they are spoken. Our words have power, much like spells do. When we speak, we have the potential to create change, influence emotions and shape reality. The words we choose impact others and carry energy and vibrations. Just like ripples in a pond, these vibrations extend outward, affecting not only others but also ourselves.

BRIDGE THAT GAP

The energy we put out through our words can attract similar energies back to us. It's like a boomerang effect; what we give out tends to come back to us in some form. Therefore, by being mindful of the energy we emit through our words, we can influence the vibrations around us.

Thoughts

Our thoughts also emit vibrations, just like our words do. What we think about influences the energy we radiate. As Dr Joe Dispenza says, 'What we think about, we bring about'. This aligns with the principles of the Law of Attraction, which suggests that positive or negative thoughts can manifest into reality. When we consistently think certain thoughts, we strengthen their vibrational frequency, making the thing we think about more potent.

These vibrations don't just disappear, they attract similar energies and experiences into our lives. They can hook onto one another, triggering related thoughts and creating a chain reaction. If we consistently direct and focus on uplifting thoughts, we emit positive vibrations and attract similar energies back to us. Conversely, negative thoughts can create negative vibrations, which can manifest and perpetuate in our daily experience. So, being aware of our thoughts is just as important as being aware of our words, as they both contribute to shaping our reality and attracting more of the same.

Emotions

Emotions are the hidden powerhouses within us, shaping every aspect of our lives. Just as our thoughts create ripples in the universe, our emotions carry their own potent energy, influencing our thoughts, actions and the world around us. Take gratitude, for instance – a vibrant, expansive emotion that ignites joy within us and sends ripples of positivity outward. When we embrace gratitude, we amplify our feel-good vibrational frequency. Conversely, negative emotions like anger, fear or resentment can cast a shadow over our day, clouding our vision. It's crucial to recognise the profound impact our emotions have and consciously choose to nurture gratitude.

Exercise

Here's a three-step approach to managing a daily gratitude journal, designed to enhance your focus:

Step 1: Morning Reflection

Start your day by reflecting on what you're grateful for. Write down three things that you feel proud and blessed about. Begin each entry with 'I am so proud and blessed of …', then list three things. These could be anything from simple joys, like the sunshine streaming through your window, to significant accomplishments or relationships.

Step 2: Setting Positive Intentions

Next, jot down three things that will make today great. This helps set a positive tone for your day and encourages you to focus on what you can look forward to. Think about specific actions, experiences or moments you'd like to create or appreciate throughout the day.

Step 3: Evening Reflection

Before you go to bed, take a moment to reflect on the events of the day. Write down three things that went well today. Celebrate your wins, no matter how small they may seem. Then, consider three things that could have been done better. Reflect on areas where you can improve or lessons you've learned. Frame these as opportunities for growth rather than criticisms.

The key to a gratitude journal is consistency and authenticity. Take a few minutes each day to reflect on your blessings, set positive intentions and review your experiences. Challenge yourself to do this for 365 days! Over time, this practice can create a major shift and attract more gratitude and positivity in your life.

The Brain's Infinite Potential: Unlocking Growth at Any Age

Expanding upon the topics covered earlier about the power of words, thoughts and emotions and the effect they have on what types of things we attract into our lives, brain adaptability, habits and routines come into focus. Our brain's ability to change and adapt plays a crucial role in shaping our habits and daily routines.

This dynamic process allows the brain to form new neural connections, strengthening existing ones, and even rewire circuits in response to various stimuli.

In children, especially young ones, brains are like sponges (heightened adaptability) soaking up new information and learning so quickly. When we were younger, our brains were highly flexible, responsive to learning and acquiring new skills, languages and knowledge at a very fast rate. As we age, the brain naturally becomes less flexible, making it more challenging to learn new things or break old habits.

Although the brain's capacity to change remains present throughout our lives, deeply ingrained patterns turn into habits and often require persistence to overcome. However, with dedication, patience and the right approach, individuals of any age can still experience growth and learning. While it may demand additional effort, the pursuit of the change you're after remains an invaluable quest worth undertaking.

Exercises that promote brain adaptability, such as engaging in the arts and music, enrich cognitive flexibility. Learning new skills, such as playing music or mastering a language, stimulates growth. Regular physical exercise, like aerobic workouts and yoga, boosts brain function. While brain training games may yield mixed results, challenging cognitive tasks are beneficial. Social engagement, processing emotional cues and other forms of interaction stimulate the brain. Visual and spatial activities foster changes in specific brain areas. Music therapy enhances auditory processing, memory and emotional regulation. Reading, puzzles and intellectual discussions provide ongoing stimulation, supporting mental growth.

With each new skill learned, each note played and each puzzle solved, we push the boundaries of transformation. The mysteries of the brain, like those of the universe, keep us in wonder. This is a great place to be, diving deeper into ourselves and marvelling at its boundless capacity for adaptation and renewal. Let us embrace the wonder of our own mental flexibility and the limitless possibilities that await us in the final frontier.

Chapter 11

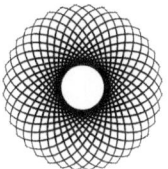

Living Legacy

A legacy is what you leave behind that lasts after you're gone, like something you created or values that have been passed down to future generations. Legacies shape the future by influencing what families do next. Cultural traditions like cooking and the way it's served and how guests in your home are treated are also legacies that are carried on. It can be a physical thing, like a painting, or something less tangible, like stories of childhood.

In today's melting pot society, culture serves as the cornerstone of our identity, fostering unity, preserving heritage and promoting social cohesion. It is through the celebration of cultural diversity, the exchange of artistic expression and the uniqueness of traditional practices that we not only enrich our lives but also cultivate a sense of belonging and understanding among communities. Actively nurturing each nationality's cultural heritage and its continuation ensures that we uphold our collective history, inspire innovation and foster a more inclusive environment in mixed nations.

My grandmother's handmade delicate doilies are our family's legacy. They're a special treasure passed down two generations so far, reminding us of our family's history and of how the women contributed to the household income by keeping their hands busy at home and the hard work they put into these intricate pieces of perfection.

Have you ever thought about what you would like to leave as your token for future generations? Even if you don't have any children of your own, what part of you would you like to leave as a symbol of your lifestyle and day-to-day musings?

No one lives forever in their physical body, so the legacy we decide to leave behind – such as the bits of our artwork, the poems and books we write and other creative items we crafted – are so profound and precious. They become tangible treasures that enrich the lives of others. It keeps us in their memories for many years to come. If the creation is nurtured and kept alive, then future generations get a glimpse of our point of view back to when it was created, creating a living legacy.

You can also leave behind a legacy through actions and traditions. It's clear that even the simplest gestures can have a lasting impact on future generations. For me, this realisation led to a deliberate effort to nurture the bonds between my children. By creating meaningful rituals and traditions, I hoped to instil a sense of connection and closeness among them. One such tradition I repeated was to gather for a monthly roast dinner, where we could share stories and cherish moments together. Additionally, I made a point to go on regular beach walks, asking the kids if they cared to join in, providing an opportunity for us to reconnect amidst their busy lives. These intentional acts were not only about fostering togetherness in the present but also about creating a legacy of love, unity and shared experiences for my children to repeat.

This book will serve as my legacy to my children. I hope it will remind them of me once I'm gone. Like Steven Covey and other prolific authors who leave behind a mountain of books, their legacy lives on as their families continue to run the business.

The biggest legacies left by leaders have sometimes changed the course of the world. Among these leaders are Marie Curie, who discovered two new chemicals and became the first woman to earn a Nobel Prize. Another is Albert Einstein, a theoretical physicist who was eccentric yet a genius. Florence Nightingale improved sanitary conditions in nursing, saving many lives; she was known to carry a pet owl during her night rounds at the hospital. Lady Diana left a powerful legacy and humanised the monarchy. She also raised awareness about mental health and bulimia, which she suffered from. I'm sure you have your own favourite legend who has left behind a living legacy that you admire.

We can take the responsibility of shaping our legacy, leaving behind a footprint that echoes for generations. It's like building a bridge between the past, present and future; a bridge built by the choices we make and the actions we take. Do we wish to keep the flame of family traditions burning bright, passing on the torch of cherished rituals and celebrations? Or perhaps we give others the opportunity, establishing scholarship funds that assist future generations to reach new heights.

BRIDGE THAT GAP

In our task to bridge our gap for a more fulfilling life, we may find comfort in the simple act of passing down our core values, anchoring the foundation of our legacy in principles of kindness, compassion and resilience. Beyond tangible assets, like a family home or a beloved vacation tradition, lies the intangible richness of our storytelling – threads of wisdom that weave through time, connecting us to our roots and nourishing our cultural identity.

Writing letters or making time capsules is a way to share stories and hopes with people from different times. When I was in primary school, I remember the whole school gathering for assembly, and the principal was opening a time capsule from previous students. I can't recall the exact age of the time capsule, but I do remember feeling fascinated and intrigued by the items that came out of it from the previous students.

Caring for the environment is a collective responsibility, making sure there's plenty of space for fun activities in the future. When we take steps to protect nature now, like keeping parks and forests clean, we're making sure that our children and grandchildren will have beautiful places to explore and enjoy. This is a gift of nature for the next generation to appreciate.

Finally, financial inheritance acts as a bridge to opportunity, providing our loved ones with the resources they need to thrive and succeed.

In each choice we make, in each action we take, we are building bridges that connect us to our past, empower us in the present and pave the way for a brighter future.

Chapter 12

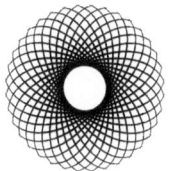

True Transformation

To achieve transformation in our external circumstances, we must first focus on transforming our inner world – our thoughts, beliefs and emotions. There must be a deep yearning, hunger, drive or obsession to begin shifting from the familiar. As I began writing this final chapter, I opened my book cabinet with nearly 300 titles to see if they would shower me with inspiration and make it easier to write this final chapter.

I found hundreds of inspirational authors, both living and dead, who chose to make a difference in readers' lives. Each book just sat there peering at me with all their beautifully designed covers, protecting the countless words inside, quivering between the pages.

BRIDGE THAT GAP

You can tell a lot about me from all the books I've purchased over the years. They represent the trials and tribulations of reshaping my inner self and manifesting significant, lasting changes in my outer world despite the stops and starts along the way.

Why does any transformation matter? Well, it doesn't! It only matters to those who are brave enough to confront their fears, insecurities and limitations. Life in and of itself is an expansion. The signs of this are in our bodies growing. But besides physical growth, true fulfilment stems from growth in all areas of life – health, wealth, relationships and contribution.

You must be okay with being vulnerable, leaving some raw wounds open for people to poke at as a catalyst for growth. In my journey, this has been through participating in exercises such as public speaking engagements where I challenged myself to speak in front of audiences, walking on hot coals as a symbolic act of breaking through my barriers and overcoming fears, volunteering at boot camps to immerse myself in physical and mental challenges, and engaging in workshops and seminars focused on personal growth and development.

These little jumps outside of your comfort zone transcend mere superficial changes or temporary fixes. If you're seeking instant gratification, you might try changing your lounge suite or buying a new model car. Material changes may offer a short burst of happiness for a few months at the most, only for you to find you are where you started – emotionally flat and looking for the next best thing shortly after.

These physical or mental challenges are powerful core-building exercises that build your trust in yourself and are vital for substantial and lasting personal inner strength. They sculpt your character, fortify your resilience and cultivate a sense of fulfilment that endures far beyond the initial discomfort.

By setting up our own little goals daily and working towards them, we experience gradient steps of achievement, contributing to a sense of satisfaction and regular wins. These incremental victories, accumulated over time, bridge the gap between our present and our desired future, allowing us to fulfil bigger goals.

Where Life Finds Meaning

In essence, life finds its meaning in serving others and enriching the world around us. This is a guiding principle that naturally extends to fulfilling our own aspirations, nurturing our spirits and fostering happiness in all we do. Ultimately, true transformation emerges when we commit to this journey of selflessness and contribution.

The concepts of *seva* in India and *sevap* in Turkish both revolve around the idea of service and kindness, albeit with some cultural nuances. In India, *seva* encompasses the selfless act of serving others without expecting anything in return. It's deeply rooted in Indian culture and spiritual traditions, emphasising the importance of compassion, empathy and altruism. On the other hand, *sevap* in Turkish carries a similar essence of kindness and goodwill towards others, but with an added dimension – the notion of earning spiritual merit or points through acts of kindness. It reflects the belief that every good deed contributes to one's spiritual growth and earns favour with a higher power.

Both concepts underscore the significance of generosity, empathy and service in fostering positive connections within communities and nurturing individual growth and fulfilment.

Seva, or acts of kindness, has far-reaching effects beyond the immediate participants, creating a ripple effect that can uplift individuals and communities alike, and it's free. Several studies in psychology and social sciences have shown that witnessing acts of kindness can have a profound impact on observers. This phenomenon is often referred to as the 'upward spiral' of positivity. When individuals witness acts of kindness, whether they are directly involved or simply observing, it can trigger a cascade of positive emotions.

One reason for this effect is that witnessing kindness can evoke feelings of empathy, compassion and altruism in observers. It can inspire them to engage in similar acts of kindness themselves, thus perpetuating a cycle of positivity. Moreover, witnessing acts of kindness can also promote a sense of social connectedness and belonging. It reminds people of the inherent goodness in humanity and brings about a sense of community and mutual support.

Additionally, research suggests that witnessing acts of kindness can have physiological benefits, reducing stress levels and promoting overall well-being. This can be attributed to the release of neurotransmitters like oxytocin, often referred to as the 'love hormone', which is associated with bonding and social connection. We all crave more of that good-feeling hormone.

As I reach the conclusion of my first book, I would like to add thought-provoking questions: How can we uncover the new set of possibilities waiting for us to step into? What versions of ourselves are patiently waiting for us to step into them? How can we connect more deeply with our authentic selves on a consistent basis, and how might that shift our perspective, experiences and, ultimately, our lives?

TRUE TRANSFORMATION

True transformation is an ongoing journey – a perpetual exploration of the massive reservoir of untapped potential residing within each of us. It's a commitment to harnessing this inherent goodness and power for the betterment of ourselves and the world around us.

Remember the old Zen saying: 'Before enlightenment, chop wood, carry water. After enlightenment, chop wood, carry water.'?

Its origins are uncertain, but its truth is clear. Enlightenment doesn't erase the ordinary, it deepens it. The tasks remain, but something shifts – presence grows, the weight of expectation lifts. And in that quiet transformation, the simplest moments become sacred.

Until we meet again, may your path be illuminated with power, purpose and prosperity.

Afterword

Dear reader,

Congratulations on completing this journey through this book! Now it's time to connect your aspirations with your actions. Think of your mind as a bridge builder. With each component, you have learned to craft your desires into reality, with gradient steps, guided by intention and belief. Remember, the journey doesn't end here; it's just the beginning.

Just imagine how much faster and further you can go with an accountability partner to support and cheer you on with each success. This is why I invite you to join me at one of my upcoming seminars or workshops.

The first step is to book a one-on-one call via the website www.BridgeThatGapBook.com to see if we can work together. We will delve deeper into conscious creation, providing practical tools to help you bridge that gap between where you are and where you aim to be.

Also, watch some interviews or listen to podcasts that I've had with some incredible thought leaders and people who are 'on' in their game.

Then, come along to live events to learn and grow

Don't let this newfound understanding remain dormant. Take action today, and let's continue this journey of growth together!

With warm regards,

Leyla Moone

About The Author

With every transformation lies a curious seeker – one dares to explore beyond the seen – and Leyla Moone is no exception. With a professional background steeped in finance, Leyla illuminates the path of self-discovery and personal reinvention through her unique techniques. For more than 30 years, she has navigated the complexities of the global financial sector, yet her true passion lies in transcending the ordinary, guiding others towards profound inner change.

Immersing herself in the teachings of Tony Robbins, Bob Proctor, Wayne Dyer, John Assaraf, Darren Hardy and so many more, Leyla has cultivated a deep understanding of the extraordinary power of the individual spirit. She believes in the boundless potential that resides within each of us, waiting to be awakened and harnessed for the next level.

With her down-to earth approach, Leyla seeks to inspire, uplift and guide readers into a deeper connection with themselves, empowering them to step fully into their potential.

Grounded in self-mastery and personal empowerment, she weaves together wisdom, insight and personal triumphs to illuminate the journey or growth and self-realisation.

Through the pages in Bridge That Gap, Leyla welcomes you into a world of limitless possibilities – unlocking the power within you. Beyond the written word, she offers workshops, speaking events and one-on-one mentoring, helping individuals and corporate teams achieve lasting change.

Step into your own transformation with Bridge That Gap, where inspiration meets action and see for yourself that the power to shift lies within you.

For more information and to begin your self-discovery journey, visit www.BridgeThatGapBook.com

References

1. From R Fritz, Your life as Art, Newfane Press, 2003; Fundamentals of Structural Thinking Workshop attended in Vermont, USA in 2012; and Creating Workshop attended in Vermont, USA in 2013.

2. T.L Rampa, You–Forever, Corgi Books, 1971.

3. N St. John, The Book of Afformations: Discovering the Missing Piece to Abundant Health, Wealth, Love, and Happiness, Hay House, Inc, 2009.

4. Christie Maree Sheldon YouTube channel, www.youtube.com/@christiemariesheldonfreetr1458.

5. T James & A James, YouTube channel, www.youtube.com/@Tad.James.

6. J Assaraf & Neurogym, https://www.myneurogym.com/.

7. S Gawain, Creative Visualisation: Use the Power of Your Imagination to Create what You Want in Your Life, New World Library, 1978.

8. J Dispenza, Breaking the Habit of Being Yourself: How to Lose Your Mind and Create a New One, Hay House, Inc, 2012.

9. E Hicks & J Hicks, YouTube channel, www.youtube.com/@Esther_Abraham_hicks_teachings.

10. Art of Living Foundation, Happiness Program, https://www.artofliving.org.

3 Offers With Calls To Action

1. Stay Connected:

Stay connected with me on social media to receive updates, exclusive content, and ongoing support in implementing the strategies discussed in this book. Join our community of like-minded individuals committed to personal growth and transformational change!

Call to Action: Follow me on Facebook Instagram and LinkedIn. Also go to my website to www.BridgeThatGapBook.com to continue your journey of Bridging that Gap sooner.

2. Apply What You've Learned:

Now that you've absorbed the wisdom shared in these pages, take the next step and apply it to your life. Diarise the exercises provided, reflect on your experiences, and start implementing positive changes to change the trajectory of your future.

Call to Action: Act today! Start by implementing one key takeaway from the book into your daily routine for it to become a habit. Share your progress and insights with us on social media using the hashtag #BridgeThatGapBook.

3. Share Your Experience:

If this book has resonated with you and helped you on your journey, please consider sharing your experience with others. Your support helps spread the message of empowerment and transformation to others who may need it right at the perfect time!

Call to Action: Leave a review on Amazon or Google Reviews, recommend it or gift it to a friend who would benefit from the techniques, or start a discussion about it in your book club or social circles.

Leyla Moone

FINANCE SPEAKER, AUTHOR, INFLUENCER

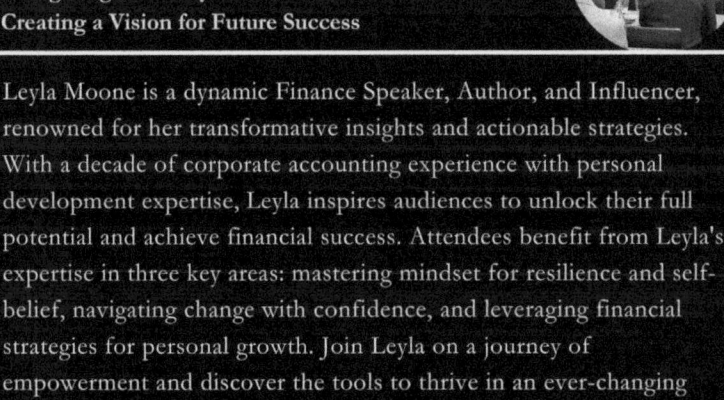

TOPICS

- Maximising Financial Strategies for Personal Growth
- Navigating Adversity with Confidence
- Creating a Vision for Future Success

Leyla Moone is a dynamic Finance Speaker, Author, and Influencer, renowned for her transformative insights and actionable strategies. With a decade of corporate accounting experience with personal development expertise, Leyla inspires audiences to unlock their full potential and achieve financial success. Attendees benefit from Leyla's expertise in three key areas: mastering mindset for resilience and self-belief, navigating change with confidence, and leveraging financial strategies for personal growth. Join Leyla on a journey of empowerment and discover the tools to thrive in an ever-changing world. Embrace possibility and unlock your future with Leyla Moone.

Testimonials
Karen sys: "saved me time and money"
Nicky says: "powerful, productive and insightful"

CONTACT

www.BrigeThatGapBook.com

facebook.com/leylamoone
instagram.com/moon8creative/
linkedin.com/in/leylaymoone/
wordpress@bridgethatgapbook.com

Notes

BRIDGE THAT GAP

NOTES

BRIDGE THAT GAP

NOTES